T0312047

Cambridge Elements

Elements in the Philosophy of Biology
edited by
Grant Ramsey
KU Leuven
Michael Ruse
Florida State University

THE METAPHYSICS OF BIOLOGY

John Dupré
University of Exeter

CAMBRIDGE
UNIVERSITY PRESS

CAMBRIDGE
UNIVERSITY PRESS

University Printing House, Cambridge CB2 8BS, United Kingdom

One Liberty Plaza, 20th Floor, New York, NY 10006, USA

477 Williamstown Road, Port Melbourne, VIC 3207, Australia

314–321, 3rd Floor, Plot 3, Splendor Forum, Jasola District Centre,
New Delhi – 110025, India

79 Anson Road, #06–04/06, Singapore 079906

Cambridge University Press is part of the University of Cambridge.

It furthers the University's mission by disseminating knowledge in the pursuit of education, learning, and research at the highest international levels of excellence.

www.cambridge.org
Information on this title: www.cambridge.org/9781009011105
DOI: 10.1017/9781009024297

© John Dupré 2021

First published 2021

A catalogue record for this publication is available from the British Library.

ISBN 978-1-009-01110-5 Paperback
ISSN 2515-1126 (online)
ISSN 2515-1118 (print)

Cambridge University Press has no responsibility for the persistence or accuracy of URLs for external or third-party internet websites referred to in this publication and does not guarantee that any content on such websites is, or will remain, accurate or appropriate.

The Metaphysics of Biology

Elements in the Philosophy of Biology

DOI: 10.1017/9781009024297
First published online: May 2021

John Dupré
University of Exeter

Author for correspondence: John Dupré, J.A.Dupre@exeter.ac.uk

Abstract: This Element is an introduction to the metaphysics of biology, a very general account of the nature of the living world. The first part of the Element addresses more traditionally philosophical questions – whether biological systems are reducible to the properties of their physical parts, causation and laws of nature, substantialist and processualist accounts of life, and the nature of biological kinds. The second half will offer an understanding of important biological entities, drawing on the earlier discussions. This division should not be taken too seriously, however: the topics in both parts are deeply interconnected. Although this does not claim to be a scientific work, it does aim to be firmly grounded in our best scientific knowledge; it is an exercise in naturalistic metaphysics. Its most distinctive feature is that argues throughout for a view of living systems as processes rather than things or, in the technical philosophical sense, substances.

Keywords: Life, Naturalistic metaphysics, Process biology, Metaphysics of science, Process ontology

ISBNs: 9781009011105 (PB), 9781009024297 (OC)
ISSNs: 2515-1126 (online), 2515-1118 (print)

Contents

Introduction

This Element might have been subtitled 'a processual perspective'. While I did initially intend to write a more impartial survey, as I began to write it became clear that it made no sense, or at least was beyond my powers, to write the Element without strongly advocating the process-centred view of the living world that I have been promoting over recent years. And as this view has yet to be universally accepted by the philosophical community, it seems only fair to alert the reader to the distinctive perspective I take on the subject matter. Of course, being opinionated doesn't mean being wrong. And I confidently anticipate that processualism will be seen as obvious by the philosophy of biology community, at least, before too long.[1] But that is, I admit, just an opinion.

This opinion also helps to shape the Element. In the first sections I take a whistle stop tour of some major themes in philosophy of science – reductionism, causation, laws of nature, mechanism, etc.– which are addressed far too briefly even to summarise the ongoing debates in these topics. I describe in somewhat greater detail the as yet less widely discussed question of whether life is composed of substances or processes. The larger part of the Element is devoted to more specific topics in biology, which are discussed in relation to these philosophical themes, especially the last. Finally, I should stress that the division into two parts should not be taken too seriously. It reflects different starting points and different debates. But in the context of the naturalistic metaphysics I espouse, it must be remembered that topics of these kinds are always mutually informing.

Part I Metaphysical Perspectives

1 What is the Metaphysics of Biology?

Metaphysics is the branch of philosophy that attempts to describe reality in the most general and abstract way. Is there only matter, for instance, or is there also mind, something essentially distinct from matter? Is the course of nature determined, or might it have gone differently? Is there a God? And so on. Traditionally, questions like this have been addressed through a priori reflection on how things must necessarily be, the nature of reality being

---

[1] Daniel Nicholson drew my attention to the following observation by JBS Haldane (1963):
'I suppose the process of acceptance will pass through the usual four stages:
1. This is worthless nonsense.
2. This is an interesting, but perverse, point of view.
3. This is true, but quite unimportant.
4. I always said so.'

exposed by the power of reason. Descartes, at the beginning of the *Meditations on First Philosophy*, planning a period of uninterrupted solitude to rebuild the foundations of his knowledge through intense reflection, provides a famous exemplar of such a methodology.

The metaphysics of biology, then, consists of the most general, abstract truths about the living world. But there is an immediate and obvious worry. As I just noted, metaphysics has traditionally been thought of as providing insight into the world through the powers of reason. But biology proceeds not by reason but by observation and experiment. If there is a fundamental difference between pigs and tables, say, surely this is something to be discovered through experience not a priori reflection on the nature of the pig? What is special about pigs is a matter for the empirical discipline of biology, not armchair reflection. Why should the *metaphysics* of biology be distinguished from the metaphysics of things or stuff more generally?

This Element presupposes a rather different view of metaphysics, however. It advocates a *naturalistic*, or scientific metaphysics. In common with a growing number of philosophers engaged with contemporary science, I take metaphysics to be a project more or less continuous with science. While its aims are more general than those of most sciences, and its methods are different, science and naturalistic metaphysics both draw essentially on experience. This will generally be experience filtered by the interpretative methods of science though sometimes it may be closer to experience as understood by common sense.

One might still ask, even granted the project of a naturalistic metaphysics, whether a metaphysics specifically of biology makes any sense. There is, after all, only one world, and it is the world of physics as well as the world of biology. Since living beings are made of physical stuff, does not the world of physics subsume that of biology? My answer to this draws on arguments I have been proposing for decades. Philosophers have tended to attach too much importance to what something is made of, a tendency that is embodied in reductionist doctrines that aim to explain the behaviour of everything by appeal to the properties, behaviour and interactions of its constituent parts and thus, ultimately, the properties and behaviour of the smallest elements of matter. But philosophers of science have increasingly rejected such doctrines as privileging matter quite inappropriately over form, or structure (Dupré 1993; Cartwright 1999).

Indeed, in my view, the metaphysics that assumes that there is in the end nothing to the world but physical particles (or fields?) and the laws of physics, is the very antithesis of a naturalistic metaphysics. A much better starting point would be to note that the various sciences differ greatly from one another not only in the entities they aim to describe, but also in their methods, instruments, social organisation and much else. To be naturalistic, therefore, both metaphysics and epistemology should, in the first instance at least, recognise this diversity. It is then unproblematic that there should be a metaphysics of *biology*, as opposed to merely a scientific metaphysics, or a metaphysics of physics. This conclusion conforms happily with the common-sense intuition that there is something (or many things) special about life, without committing to a far more problematic idea, the vitalism that holds living things to be made of, or partly made of, something quite distinct from ordinary matter.

The aim of this Element, then, will be to articulate a picture of what it is to be living by drawing on the deliverances of our best science. Science, as everyone knows, is fallible. The best science of today may be the phlogiston or caloric fluid of tomorrow. So this must be a fallibilist metaphysics. This again sharply distinguishes the naturalistic metaphysics explored here from the traditional rationalist version that is generally taken to consist of truths that are both a priori and necessary. If such a metaphysical view is false, the failure to see it as such can be attributed only to the limits of human reason. For a naturalistic metaphysics, a view may be wrong despite being the most rational conclusion to draw from the current state of scientific opinion, as may appear when our empirical understanding advances. As a matter of fact, I think that biology has progressed to a point where its basic outlines are sufficiently secure to provide the grounding for a compelling biological metaphysics. A metaphysics that is grounded in science, however, must share the insecurity of its foundations. And as limited beings in a world of almost limitless complexity this is a predicament that we should learn to live with (Wimsatt 2007).

2 Reductionism, Emergence and Levels of Organisation

In this section I will pursue a little further the question of whether biology could be genuinely autonomous from physics and chemistry in a way that would provide a more permanent license for an independent metaphysics of biology. Is biology, in principle at least, reducible to the physical sciences, or might biological properties rather be *emergent* – appearing in novel ways at higher levels of organisation, so that no knowledge of the properties of constituent parts is sufficient in principle for predicting such properties. If this is not the case, if we anticipate ultimately reducing biology to very complex problems in physics and chemistry, or even if we think that such a reduction is possible, but only for beings with intellectual powers greater than ours, then the metaphysics of biology will look provisional, or at least shallow. There will be nothing to it in principle beyond a metaphysics grounded solely in the physical sciences.

An argument that continues to motivate the reductionist view goes as follows. Suppose that physics is causally complete, in the sense that a full knowledge of the laws governing the behaviour of whatever are the ultimate (smallest) constituents of the world will show that behaviour to be fully determined by the preceding state of those constituents. In that case, any macroscopic object entirely composed of these constituents will have its behaviour fully determined by these same laws. Suppose, for example, I decide to scratch my nose. Very large numbers of physical particles are elevated from their various positions alongside my torso, and those that constitute my index finger move up and down in the immediate vicinity of my nose. All these movements, *ex hypothesi*, are predictable from the laws of physics. Hence the appearance that something like my decision or will caused this movement is, at best, redundant, since it was also fully caused by the laws of physics applied to my constituent parts.[2]

In response to this, and other reductionist intuitions, there is an extensive literature on emergence, both in philosophy of science and in analytic metaphysics. Wilson (2016) reviews a good part of this, and provides a painstaking analysis of arguments of the kind just sketched, and the possible strategies for resisting them. My own view is that we have good reason to reject the assumption of the causal completeness of physics, the key premise of this reductionist argument (e.g. Dupré 1993, pp. 99–102). Of course, as a naturalist, if physics were to start explaining the behaviour of complex systems such as organisms on the basis of fundamental physics I would begin to question this belief. But equally, in the absence of any such remarkable achievements or any prospect of them in the foreseeable future, a naturalist should resist such a priori convictions about the future trajectory of science. Although we should be generally agnostic about the future of science, it is reasonable to expect some modicum of continuity between the kinds of results science has achieved to date, and what it may be expected to accomplish in the future. The idea that fundamental physics might some day, or could in principle, fully explain or predict the behaviour of a duck or a dolphin surely violates this condition.

In recent years, philosophers of biology have tended strongly towards the rejection of reductionism and the acceptance of some kind of emergence, and this conclusion has been sufficiently widespread to legitimate an autonomous and naturalistic metaphysics of biology. But there remains a great deal of debate about exactly what this failure of reductionism amounts to. Is it just a practical problem of too much complexity, although the underlying reality remains purely physical and purely determined by physical law? Are

---

[2] Arguments of this sort have been developed and discussed in greatest detail by Jaegwon Kim (e.g. 2000).

emergent properties merely, for example, reflections of the impossibility of deriving a property without tracing every step in the course of its appearance (Bedau 1997), or do they reflect something more radically new (Humphreys 2016)?

My own conviction is that emergence is indeed something metaphysically robust. I shall not, however, attempt to argue for this right away. In the next section I shall say a little about causation and especially so-called 'downward causation', a phenomenon which, if it exists, clearly contradicts reductionism. In Section 4, in which I explain the contrast between an ontology of things and one of processes, and explain why the latter must be preferred for biology, it will become clearer why I think downward causation is something that happens all the time and, hence, why emergence is everywhere.

I will mention here just one further reason for suspicion of reductionism. Reductionism conflates claims about the world (properties of organisms are determined by properties of their parts) with claims about scientific representations of the world (biological theories are derivable from physical theories). But the move from the first of these claims to the second is permissible only if there is a strong correspondence between the two, that is, if scientific representations are (or aim to be) simply complete descriptions of the phenomena. But science, or at least biological science, it is now widely believed, works mainly by generating models of real phenomena, and these models idealise or abstract from many details of the target that are judged of minor significance for the use to which the models are to be put. Thus, scientific models do not provide, or even aim to provide, the whole and complete truth about the world. Hence, even a successful a priori argument that the properties of a complex whole depend in some sense on the properties of its parts is insufficient to show that the best model of the whole is related in any particular way to the best models of its parts.

There are philosophers who will be unconcerned by the fact that science fails to support the completeness of physics and the consequent truth of reductionism at least in principle, taking these to be intuitively obvious or demonstrable via some kind of a priori argument. Here I can only reassert my commitment to a naturalistic metaphysics, and hence the view that a priori argument cannot be the right way to find out what the world is like. I can imagine no reason why our experience should not be of a world with very limited regularity that admitted of no inference to complete physical laws. Only empirical investigation can tell us whether we live in such a world or whether we live in a world shaped only by physical law. And, as I shall try to explain further over the next two sections, I think there is a great deal of empirical reason for rejecting the latter view.

I wrote at the beginning of this section of levels of organisation. What are these? It is common to think of levels in terms of the subject matters of different sciences: physics, chemistry, biology, sociology, say, providing a sequence of progressively higher levels. Science textbooks often present us with a neat hierarchical picture of the world, where societies are built from individual organisms, which are built out of cells, and so on down to subatomic particles.

But of course, this is very simplistic. Physics, for a start, considers stars and galaxies as well as quarks and photons, so if levels are thought of in terms of physical size, they cannot be correlated with traditional disciplines. Second, the boundaries between members of this hierarchy are not clear: where do physical chemistry, or biochemistry, or molecular biology belong? And third, many actual areas of scientific enquiry involve elements from many different levels. Consider cell biology. Cells contain functional elements as small as ions, including hydrogen ions, or protons, often supposed to be within the remit of particle physics. They also contain very large molecules, structures of molecules such as membranes or organelles, and even sometimes organisms, such as endosymbiotic bacteria. Or consider the growing use of biophysical models in developmental biology, as do Green and Batterman (2017), in a related antireductionist argument.

In short, talk of levels should not be taken too seriously. It is useful on occasion to have a word to refer to the relations between, for example, cells and tissues, or organs and organisms, but one should treat such a word with caution. In particular, we should be careful not to take the common application of levels talk to cases such as the preceding to imply that there is anything important in common between such cases. This would be a highly questionable conclusion, but it is one that is often implicit in discussions of reductionism and emergence. At any rate, when I speak of levels of organisation I mean to refer only to a part-whole relation that has explanatory utility in a particular context. I do not mean to imply that there is some objectively determinate set of such levels in nature.

3 Causation, Laws, Mechanisms and Models

The question of reductionism or emergence, and whether the latter is merely an epistemological problem or reflects the genuine appearance of something more than the sum of its parts, is deeply embedded in a set of interconnected issues in the metaphysics of science, and the gradual decline of belief in reductionism must be understood in relation to a number of developments in these related topics. Focal among these topics is the metaphysics of causation. Whereas not long ago causation was widely understood as involving sequences of events instantiating universal laws, in the philosophy of biology the concept of law has been largely abandoned, and replaced by an analysis of scientific understanding through models. Causation, in turn, has increasingly been explained as the operation of a mechanism.

One question of immediate relevance to our present concerns is the possibility of downwards causation, the causal influence of wholes on their parts. If this occurs, then it seems impossible to sustain the idea that all that really exists is what constitutes the simplest physical level. For if the behaviour of entities at that smallest level must be causally explained by appeal to entities at higher levels, the lowest level is incapable of providing a complete account of reality. In this section, I will say more about these broad developments in the philosophy of causality and their relevance to our understanding of biological causation. While I think that the concern with mechanism in recent philosophy of the life sciences has been generally salutary, I shall conclude that its metaphysical payoff is limited. Mechanisms are always to some degree abstractions from the processes that constitute living systems. These processes will be the topic of the next section.

Discussions of causation standardly begin with Hume's famous arguments against causal powers or causal necessity and his conclusion that causation resides only in the regularity of association between occurrences of certain kinds, associations commonly interpreted as laws of nature. Subsequent philosophers have divided between enthusiastic followers of Hume's position (e.g. Mill 1872/1843; Mackie 1974) and attempts, *pace* Hume, to revive theories based on powers residing in objects (e.g. Harré and Madden 1975; Mumford and Anjum 2011). Accounts of the first kind may also be taken to include counterfactual theories (causes as that without which an effect would not have occurred) (Lewis 1973), and the influential difference-making account of Woodward (2003)[3]. Accounts of the second kind have recently evolved into theories centred on mechanisms (Glennan 1996; Machamer, Darden and Craver 2000) or on processes (Salmon 1984, Dupré 2013).

A tendency, at least among naturalistically inclined philosophers, to move towards positions on the anti-Humean side of this dichotomy, has been motivated in part by a decline in the perceived importance of scientific laws. Highly influential work by Nancy Cartwright (1983) has led many to doubt whether even physics could generate true universal laws. There has been a good deal of talk of laws being probabilistic rather than deterministic, but it has proved very difficult to show that these were universal (x% of As cause Bs) rather than merely the outcome of capacities (As can cause Bs) in a particular set of

---

[3] But see note 6, below.

background conditions (Dupré 1993, ch. 9). Philosophers of biology have been increasingly ready to agree that there may at least be no general laws in the life sciences (e.g. Brandon 1997; Beatty 1995). Both consequent on and contributing to this growing scepticism about laws has been a rapidly increasing emphasis on the construction of models (e.g. Lloyd 1988).[4]

Laws of nature were traditionally understood as strictly true of the world. Of course, actual events often or even generally did not occur in exact accordance with any such laws, because there would almost always be other factors interfering: the world is very complex and there are typically many things going on at any one time and place. But the laws were held to be true *ceteris paribus*, or perhaps *ceteris absentibus*. No one, on the other hand, supposes that a model must be exactly identical to the thing of which it is a model. Borges's (1998) famous story of the perfect map – exactly the size of the territory mapped, and including every detail – and its perfect uselessness nicely illustrates the point. Models, as I have already mentioned in connection with reductionism, abstract or idealise. They may be known to be false, including non-existent entities such as frictionless planes and point masses, or to be incomplete, as in ecological models that only describe the behaviour and interactions of a small number of supposedly crucial species. So how do models represent causality?

Given the extent of the recent literature on models in the philosophy of the life sciences I can only offer a very superficial answer to this last question.[5] But what I think is clear is that the emphasis on models signals, even if it does not strictly require, a strongly anti-Humean direction in the philosophy of causation. Most models do not provide understanding by subsumption under universal regularities but, at least in a central class of cases, by showing how a range of factors or entities exercise capacities that together tend to produce the phenomenon to be explained. In a subclass of these cases, the factors involved are components of the entity whose behaviour is to be explained, structured in a particular way. These are the cases that have been very widely discussed in recent philosophy under the rubric of mechanism (Machamer, Darden and Craver 2000; Glennan 1996).

Generally, mechanist philosophers take real mechanisms in the world to be the referents of such models, though there are significant differences in views

---

[4] This is sometimes discussed in terms of a move from the syntactic to the semantic view of theories; one may also distinguish a third, pragmatic view, that recognises a more complex and diverse array of constituents that may form parts of theories (Winther 2016).

[5] There is an extensive recent philosophical literature on models (Frigg and Hartmann 2018; Weisberg 2012; Toon 2012). It is also clear that there are many kinds of models. I don't discuss, for example, material models, which are very important in biology in the guise of model organisms (Ankeny and Leonelli 2011).

about the relation between model and mechanism. Just as the parts of a washing machine or a lawnmower are organised in ways that explain why their operation causes clothes to become cleaner or blades of grass shorter, so, it is said, the parts of the heart are organised so that their various capacities interact to cause blood to be circulated around the animal body. The heart is a mechanism which the model describes. A model of the heart, then, might consist of more or less idealised representations of key components – valves, chambers, etc. – and show how these combine to move the blood through the whole. These representations will not, at any rate, be identical in all respects to any actual valve or chamber and many less important features of actual hearts will not be included in such a model.

In addition, scientists often manipulate models as a way of exploring properties of the objects the models are intended to represent (see, e.g., Morgan 1999; Toon 2012, ch. 5). The variety of manipulations echoes the diversity of models. Model organisms may be experimentally manipulated; mathematical models may have particular variables manipulated. In many such cases the effect on the model of the manipulation is intended to disclose the causal capacity of some part or feature of the target isomorphic with the manipulated feature of the model. This idea naturally aligns with the interventionist account of causation (Woodward 2003).[6]

There is no doubt that such a mechanistic strategy has been highly successful in the life sciences, and provides a credible interpretation of the dominant role of mechanistic models in this domain. And this success provides the basis for a compelling argument that such sciences call for a capacity-centred view of causation. Some enthusiasts for the approach want to go further, and claim that the success of mechanistic research in biology shows that biological entities really *are* mechanisms. I shall say more about this view shortly, but first I want to return to the topic of downward causation. For if there is downward causation, causation that acts from wholes on the parts of which they are composed, then surely parts do not *fully* explain causally the behaviour of wholes, even if models of interacting parts provide important explanations of behaviour in appropriate circumstances.

The idea of downwards causation must be treated with caution. Is it to be contrasted with upwards causation? What could that be? On one interpretation of the reductionist hypothesis, if it is true, the lower level cannot causally influence the upper level, since this hypothesis proposes a world in which there is no upper level to influence. Recall, however, my initial description of

---

[6] Thus, incidentally, problematizing my classification of causal theories above into Humean and non-Humean. For more detailed discussion of many of the issues above, including the relation of mechanisms to laws and to models, see Craver and Tabery (2019).

models above, as (sometimes) showing how a range of factors or entities exercise capacities that together tend to produce a phenomenon to be explained. Suppose we think of the phenomenon as the behaviour of some entity, and of all such factors as causes of the phenomenon. Then, without any commitment to levels, we may simply define upward causation as including all those cases where the factor is a component of the entity exhibiting the behaviour, and downward causation will apply to cases in which the causal factor is an entity of which the entity whose behaviour is to be explained is a constituent part. Downward causation, then, provides the explanatory converse of mechanistic explanation, the explanation of the behaviour of some component of a model by appeal to the action of the whole. Note that I have framed this description of downward causation in terms of *explanation*: it describes explanation, at least, as running from whole to part as well as from part to whole. How does this get us to downward *causation*? Scientific explanations, we often suppose, get their strength from mapping casual relations. So, if there are such downward explanations, can they be properly construed as pointing to downward causal relations?

Take a simple example of such an explanation. Why did my elbow elevate twelve feet? Because I walked upstairs to my bedroom and, as usual, I took my elbow with me. The exercise of my capacity to climb stairs explains my elbow's being on the first floor. Of course, a reductionist will deny that the influence of the whole (myself) over the parts is properly causal. The real causal explanation is that certain events in my brain generated electrical impulses that activated the muscles in my legs in certain ways, and rigid connections of my legs and arms to my spine transferred forces from my legs to my arms, and so on. The whole organism plays no essential part in the story. How might it do so?

The beginning of an answer is that in many biological cases the capacity of the part is itself necessarily dependent on the whole. It is not just that properties or capacities of parts explain capacities or behaviour of the whole, but that explanation runs in the opposite direction as well. The capacity of my muscles to move my legs depends on their embedding in the larger system, me. The mechanist will of course reply that the same is true for mechanical parts: the piston only has the capacity to direct the force of an explosion when it is embedded in a cylinder, and much else besides. But biological entities have a much deeper dependency on their context, which I can only describe fully when I talk about process in Section 4. But to summarise the position I shall defend there, the muscle is not a thing that has the relevant capacity, when connected to other things in the right way; rather it is a process that would not exist at all, if it were not stabilised by the proper functioning of the whole. Without the constant provision of blood, oxygen, etc., to the muscle by the whole system, it would not merely lack the capacity to contract, it would not exist at all. So, my capacity to go upstairs is not reducible to the capacities of structural parts; both the capacities of the parts and their very existence as the kinds of parts they are depend on the whole organism. So, finally, the capacity of the whole organism to ascend the stairs is an irreducible capacity of the organism, and there is no reason to doubt that the explanation of the movement of my parts is made true by facts that may unobjectionably be referred to as downward causation.

Craver and Bechtel (2007) object to all talk of upward and downward causation, preferring to account for the relevant phenomena in terms of intra-level causation and mechanical mediation of effects. This idea depends on the identity of a whole (mechanism) to the properly organised sum of its parts. The explanation of my elbow's ascent is that it is a part of the mechanism the totality of which is me. So, there is a mechanistic explanation of how the movements of my legs propel me (the whole mechanism) up the stairs, and my elbow, being part of me, comes along for the ride. This interpretation assumes, however, that there is always a sufficient mechanistic explanation, the assumption, explicit in Craver and Bechtel's paper, that 'all higher-level causes are fully explained by constitutive mechanisms' (Craver and Bechtel 2007, p. 248). This is just a denial that we have any need for top-down explanation, and hence any motivation for appealing to downward causation.

Applying the proposition that 'all higher-level causes are fully explained by constitutive mechanisms' in the obvious way to the case of my going upstairs points to a quite different problem with the reductive mechanistic position. The claim is that my mounting the stairs is fully explained by a hierarchy of events or processes inside my body; my ascent of the stairs then 'mechanically mediates' the elevation of my elbow. One should then object that the explanation of my going upstairs is very likely a consequence of my embedding in some much larger system. A friend has asked me to find a document that I believe is somewhere in my study, for example. Then a sufficient explanation of my action includes entities outside my body, in this case my friend. Why did my friend want the document? It is easy to see how the relevant factors could be multiplied indefinitely. This is the kind of possibility that, it seems, Craver and Bechtel's assumption must either exclude by fiat, or accommodate trivially, merely by including my friend in the mechanism of which I and she are both constitutive parts. If the whole universe is a mechanistic system, then every-thing that happens could be seen as mechanically mediated by the running of the universe.

This is a general problem for reductionist positions. Reductionism can only apply fully to closed systems, but there are no closed systems, at least in biology.

Every biological system depends for its continued existence on constant inter-action with its environment. What would be a non-reductionist interpretation of this tendency for explanations to flow beyond the bounds of their target systems? It seems that we need an approach much more pragmatic than the search for an explanation isomorphic to an underlying causal reality. The problem with such an approach is that it is often taken to involve some kind of anti-realism, the severing of the proper connection between the explanation and facts in the world. I suggest that a pragmatic rejection of the unique and exhaustive underlying causal reality, together with a robust connection between explanation and reality, can be understood along the following lines.

The reductionist's world is an ordered world. Everything happens for a reason, or at least a sufficient cause, and explanations of events are good in proportion to how much of this underlying cause they capture. But this ordered world is at best an object of faith (Dupré 1993). The world might equally well be highly disordered, with the little bits of order we encounter, most notably living systems, rare and precious exceptions. As I shall explain in the next section, one way of articulating an account of such a world is as consisting of temporarily ordered structures, what we often describe as 'things', in a flux of largely disordered process. 'As process ontologists see it, enduring things are never more than patterns of stability in a sea of process' (Rescher 2006, p. 14). The stabilisation of these things, at least in the familiar biological case, requires a range of activities both in the systems ('mechanisms') that make up the thing, and in the larger systems in which they are embedded. Changes, or for that matter persistences, in a thing may appeal to any of these activities, which may be the only, or the dominant, factor at work. So such explanations may certainly point to real features of the world; but they do not locate the precise place of a phenomenon in the order of things, for there is no such order and hence no such place.

I will lead into the discussion of process with a few further remarks on the so-called new mechanism introduced in the already mentioned and extremely influential paper by Machamer, Darden and Craver (2000) (hereafter MDC).[7] This movement has proposed that describing mechanisms is the pre-eminent form of explanation in the life sciences, and that mechanisms are what underlie causal relations. Some mechanists also take an ontological, or metaphysical view of mechanism, asserting that living systems just are mechanisms, and mechanisms made of further, smaller mechanisms. To understand this we need to consider a bit further what, exactly, a mechanism is.

---

[7] While MDC is widely identified as the take-off point for this movement, earlier work promoted the importance of mechanism, notably by Stuart Glennan (1996).

MDC define a mechanism like this: 'Mechanisms are entities and activities organized such that they are productive of regular changes from start or set-up to finish or termination conditions' (2000, p. 3). As MDC explicitly acknowledge, this is a dualistic definition. There are two constituents to a mechanism, entities and their activities. An activity, moreover, requires an entity that performs or executes it. Whether the relation to machines implicit in the term 'mechanism' is to be taken literally (the biological systems modelled mechanistically just *are* machines) or more analogically,[8] it is easy to see how this picture fits a machine. For a classical machine, at any rate, say the excellent crank and screw-driven apple peeler, slicer and corer, the parts may sit inactive though linked in my kitchen drawer for years on end. Then I *impale* an apple with the spikes on the shaft and *turn* the handle, and the blades *cut out* strips of skin, *slice* the apple into a continuous spiral and excise the core. The entities (spikes, handle, blades), impale, slice, etc. There are no slicings without blades or equivalents that do the slicing.

The analogy with biological systems is problematic, however. It can, of course, be illuminating to treat the heart as a pump, with suitably arranged contracting and expanding chambers and valves, but the analogy with a machine is limited. Hearts cannot sit unused in drawers. As is all too familiar, a heart that stops acting for even a few minutes may be fatally damaged. There are indeed no contractions without contracting chambers. But it is also a causal truth, at least, that there are no chambers without contractions. Contractions are necessary to provide the flow of oxygenated blood to the heart muscle tissue without which in a very short time it loses its capacity to function. Such causal dependence of the entity on its activity is characteristic of all biological systems, and is at the centre of why, in the next section, I shall argue that such systems are processes rather than things, or substances.

If there is a dualism of entities and activities, it is not an egalitarian dualism. Activities are more fundamental and it is not the case that an activity requires an entity to carry it out, unless we simply define an entity as whatever stuff is involved in the activity. Consider a storm. There is no pre-existing entity that is constituted by the water and air that comes to make up a storm. The constituents are part of a storm because there is a storm tying them together, so to speak, and indeed the constituents of the storm will change rapidly as the storm develops and moves. The storm is a process that takes in bits of matter that are, for a time, parts of it. Just the same should be said of a heart or an elephant. Or so I shall argue in the next section.

---

[8] Craver (2007, p. 4) explicitly distinguishes a mechanism from a machine.

Philosophy of Biology

4 Things and Processes

Perhaps the oldest debate in Western philosophy is that between those who think we live in a world of change, and those who see the world as fundamentally stable. In the starkest version of this opposition we have Heraclitus famously asserting that everything changes, and Parmenides equally well known for the view that nothing changes. The Parmenidean claim seems prima facie absurd, as we see things changing all around is, but takes on a more plausible guise in the view of atomists, most notably Democritus. For atomism, the real constituents of the universe are eternal and intrinsically unchanging atoms. The only real changes are the rearrangements and changing spatial relations of these, but this activity creates the impressions of macroscopic objects and changes that these undergo. This is the worldview that eventually came to dominate scientific thinking from the seventeenth century onwards.

The view that I want to urge is that this atomistic turn was a major mistake for biology, and we would have done better to follow a Heraclitean approach to the study of life (Dupré and Nicholson 2018). Heraclitus is most famous for the rather curious opinion that you cannot step into the same river twice, though a more useful version runs 'You never step into the same river twice, for it's not the same river and you're not the same person'. There are actually two interpretations of the shorter version, deriving from a well-known ambiguity in the word 'same'. If 'same' means just the same thing, what philosophers call *numerical* identity, the claim seems plainly wrong. I can step in the Thames today and again tomorrow, and thereby step into the same river twice. The longer quote, on the other hand, suggests that what is meant is rather *qualitative* identity. And then the claim seems almost trivial. I am not exactly the same weight as I was yesterday, and I will have shed skin cells, acquired memories, and so on; and much the same applies to the river.

I said 'almost' trivial, because while it seems plainly true for the particular case – humans and rivers – it is not obviously true for more stable entities. Can I sit in the same chair twice? The question in view is now what it is for something to persist through time, and it appears at first sight that something like a river, or a human, can't do that because they are constantly changing, while perhaps a chair can. Does this mean that I am wrong to think I can step in the Thames on different days? Or, far more plausibly, should we suspect that we have an inappropriate conception of persistence through time? I am not qualitatively the same man as yesterday, but surely that doesn't mean I am not numerically the same man?

Before pursuing this question, we should reinterpret the worlds of change and of stasis as worlds of process and of things. But before doing this we must address a difficult terminological issue. The philosophical tradition has spoken most often not of things, but of substances. But this word has two serious problems. First, everyday language means something quite specific and quite different from the philosophical usage by 'substance', namely a kind of stuff. So the word can mislead the casual reader. Second, the philosophical tradition has meant multiple different things by substance. Standard characteristics of substances include: being ontologically basic; being relatively independent and durable; being subjects of predication, or subjects of change; being kinds of objects, or kinds of stuff (Robinson 2020). For both these reasons I shall avoid the word 'substance' and contrast processes, instead, with *things*. But inevitably, my usage will not be exactly as that word is commonly meant. As I use the word, a thing is relatively independent and durable, has reasonably clear boundaries and it does not overlap with, though it may contain, other things. My things are also the subjects of knowledge. To know about a domain is to know what things it contains, what properties they have, and how they behave. And importantly, a thing is an entity the default state of which is stasis. If it changes this is because something interacts with it, or something changes within it; its changes call for explanation. Finally, this description is intended to be fairly loose, but not indefinitely so. In particular, it should exclude things whose boundaries are too vague to be useful subjects of knowledge. A mountain range may be a thing, but a mountain is usually not, as the division of a range into individual mountains involves arbitrary decisions. The majority of philosophers, both historically and in the present, have taken it that we live in a world of things, more or less meeting these conditions. In such a world there are processes, but they are sequences of changes that things undergo; things are thus ontologically prior: there could not be processes if there were no things.

A process, on the other hand, is either simply a sequence of changes, or it is an arrangement of matter that cannot persist without undergoing changes. A classic example is an eddy in a river, maintained by the flow that surrounds it. Or consider an animal. For it to continue being the animal it is a vast number of activities must be occurring: the heart beats; haemoglobin molecules pick up oxygen; genes are transcribed and translated; metabolic reactions are catalysed; and so on. An animal in which nothing is happening must be dead and probably deep frozen. A process ontology can, of course, explain the appearance of permanent 'things': they are structures maintained by underlying activities. To repeat an earlier quote from Nicholas Rescher: 'As process ontologists see it, enduring things are never more than patterns of stability in a sea of process' (Rescher 2006). So the processes are ontologically prior to the things.

It might seem obvious that there must be things, that processes must be made of something, and hence things are more fundamental than processes. A pervasive annoyance in the exposition of a processualist position is that it is almost impossible to avoid words such as 'something', 'anything' or 'everything', and indeed 'thing' itself. But these words assume a much broader sense of 'thing' than that in question in this metaphysical debate. The something that processes must be made of need not be composed of things, as atomists have held, but can merely be stuff. Both processes and things must, perhaps, be made of some kind of stuff. But this stuff might be made of things, it might be entirely homogeneous, or it might be the manifestation of an underlying process. Since my concern is with biology rather than physics, I do not propose to debate the nature of the ultimate stuff of reality, and my view of biological process is even consistent with an underlying atomism. It is important, however, that the possibility of entities, whether whales or photons, being the manifestation of process rather than the aggregation of things, is not ruled out a priori. Even if the ultimate physical constituents of the world are indeed persisting things,[9] so that biological processes are ultimately composed of things, there may be no (unified, persistent, unchanging) thing which undergoes the process that is an elephant or an oak tree. Just as for the storm, even if the stuff of which it is composed is ultimately an aggregation of things (atoms), there is no thing composed of these constituents.

So let us now return to the question of persistence over time.[10] There is a common temptation to conflate qualitative and numerical identity, but philosophers have learned to resist it. While there may be classical atoms that are completely unchanging and for which, therefore, qualitative and numerical identity coincide, macroscopic things are not so well-behaved. Even the standard exemplars of things, tables and chairs, or J. L. Austin's famous 'moderate-sized specimens of dry goods' (Austin 1962, p. 8), will shed the odd molecule, or acquire ingrained deposits of dust, dead insects and suchlike. In response to this problem, the traditional philosophical response has been to attribute essential properties to a thing, properties the continued possession of which are necessary and sufficient for the continued existence of the thing. Normally, essential properties pertain to a thing as members of a kind for which the property provides a condition of membership, and it is widely supposed that to be the same thing over time an entity must belong to, and continue to belong to, a particular kind. As I shall discuss in the next section, however, it is widely

---

[9] It does, in fact, seem to me that there is a great deal in modern physics that cries out for interpretation in terms of process. But as noted in the text, this is not the place to debate this issue.

[10] This topic is addressed from the points of view of both traditional metaphysics and the philosophy of biology in Meincke and Dupré (2020).

agreed that the empirical facts of biology are not consistent with there being any such essence-determined kinds.

But persistence of a process is a rather different problem[11]. By definition, for a start, no process can persist without change. But, second, the question of process continuity should not be decided by comparing two stages, and seeing if they are similar in the right ways, but is rather a question of there being the right kinds of relations between those stages, namely causal continuity. This can readily be illustrated with the case of an animal. There need be no property that makes it the case that an egg and a frog are stages in the life cycle of the same animal; what is needed is the right kind of causal history. This has been dubbed 'genidentity' (Lewin 1922; Pradeu 2018). Someone might suppose that some property like genome sequence might do the first kind of job. As a matter of fact, I don't think this could work. Genes are much more fluid and mutable than people often assume (Dupré 2012, chs. 6, 7). But the crucial point is that it doesn't have to work. Causal continuity of process understood in this way is consistent with any property of an early stage ceasing to apply to a later stage.

A third point is particularly important. Identity of things has always been understood as an all or nothing question, applying, when it does, to exactly all the things that happen to exist. Identity of processes is a much less determinate matter. Think of the iconic exemplar of a process, a river. Is the Mississippi system one river, or one river the Mississippi and a tributary, the Missouri?[12] If the latter, then are the lesser tributaries, the Ohio, the Arkansas, and so on, also not part of the Mississippi? And, if so, how big does a stream flowing into a river have to be to be a separate entity? Similarly, how wide does the river have to be to become a lake? And for all these cases, where exactly are the boundaries, between a river and its tributary, or a river and the lake into which it flows? I take it the answers to all of these questions are more or less indeterminate, pointing to the fact that dividing interconnected processes into distinct individuals is seldom if ever a question fully determined by objective facts.[13] But note that this should not lead us to the conclusion that there are no such individuals. Whatever the answers to the preceding questions, it makes perfect sense, and is entirely natural, to say that the Thames at Oxford and the Thames at London are the same river; or the Thames I stepped into yesterday is the same river as the

---

[11] For a process-centred account of persistence, see Meincke (2019).

[12] Why the latter rather than one river, the Lower and Middle Mississippi and the Missouri, and a tributary, the Upper Mississippi? The Missouri is longer than the Upper Mississippi, though it carries less water. Which is the more appropriate criterion?

[13] If I had not excluded such vague entities as mountains from my category of things, much the same might have been said of them. How big must a saddle be between two peaks to constitute two distinct mountains, or when does a hill count as a mountain? If a mountain does count as a thing, then some things are in this respect more like processes than most people have thought.

Thames I stepped into today. The flow of water connects Oxford and London, and the flow has continued since yesterday. As I shall explain in Section 8, such partially indeterminate boundaries are exactly what we find in organisms, and this is one of the indications that these are better understood as processes than as things.

I shall conclude this section by noting that for some philosophers in the mainstream tradition of analytic metaphysics, this rejection of substance in favour of process is wrong-headed if not incoherent. Probably the most influential exponent of the concept of substance in recent philosophy has been David Wiggins, and he has explicitly criticised the kind of processual proposal that I advocate (Wiggins 2016).[14]

It seems to me, to get straight to the point, that much of Wiggins's objection is built into his conceptual framework from the start. He distinguishes processes from *continuants* in the following way:

> Continuants exist in time, have material parts and pass through phases. But such phases are not the material parts of the continuant. The phases are parts of the continuant's span of existence. Contrast processes. The phases of a particular historically dateable process are its parts (2016, 270).

In common with much standard metaphysical theory, Wiggins is here distinguishing two ways of persisting, often referred to as enduring and perduring. Continuants endure. They do not have temporal parts, because they are 'wholly present' whenever they exist at all. So instead they have 'phases'. A process, on the other hand, perdures. It is the sum of its temporal parts and so only part of a process is present at any time. An organism is a substance and a continuant, and endures, so it cannot be a process.[15]

I should note that Wiggins has made more effort than any substance theorist I know of (at least since Aristotle) to develop the concept of a substance in a way that is amenable to the peculiar features of organisms. Nonetheless, I think that the framework he advocates is ill-suited to describing the living world. Certainly, an organism has material parts; but I see no reason to legislate that it cannot, therefore, also have temporal parts. The idea that a substance is 'wholly present' at any one time is most familiar in debates about personal identity, but it is intended to apply to any substance, and

---

[14] This paper also criticises the use of the concept of genidentity developed for similar antisubstantialist purposes with respect to biology by Guay and Pradeu (2015b).

[15] There is some debate among metaphysicians about this standard conception of processes. Rowland Stout (2016) defends the category of continuant processes. Helen Steward has defended the traditional distinction in several places (e.g. and with special reference to the ideas defended here, in Steward (2020)). Meincke (2019) argues that a satisfactory account of identity through change *requires* the category of continuant processes.

certainly any organism.[16] I'm not sure whether I understand what it is to be wholly (or partly) present. But it strikes me as a misleading thing to say – misleading, at any rate, in any situation where there is reason to say it – that an organism is wholly present.

In many scientific contexts, it is crucial to know that this is only one stage in the life history of the organism, and what it is and does will vary greatly according to what stage the organism has reached. That it is the kind of entity that has these other stages may be crucial to its proper understanding. Indeed, stages of an organism have often been originally misclassified as members of unrelated species. Wiggins will not be concerned by this. For him these stages belong to the life history of an organism, but not to the organism itself. But of course, the distinction between an organism and its life history is exactly what a processual understanding of an organism denies. The organism just is its life history; and hence it is at best highly misleading to claim that it is wholly present at any one stage of its life cycle. I don't take the preceding two paragraphs to constitute an argument against Wiggins's view, only to show that his conceptual scheme rules out a process view of the organism from the start. Arguments for the latter will come in a later section.

Wiggins also argues that organism talk could not be replaced by process talk, and that this is evident in the different attributions that can be applied to processes and continuants:

> But how is talk of organisms to be replaced altogether by talk of processes which submit to attributions such as rapid, regular, staccato, steady or cyclical? Organisms themselves cannot submit to these attributions. (2016, 270)

Rivers can be rapid or steady, suggesting that they are processes and thus examples of apparently continuant processes. Indeed, so can organisms. Wiggins might reply that a cheetah is not rapid *tout court*, but (sometimes) runs rapidly. (And a seal, say, may swim rapidly but move slowly on dry land.) It is somehow implicit in our understanding of a river that if it is rapid what it does rapidly is flow. But of course I do not want to deny that there are different kinds of processes, and that some (simple) processes may have their activities analytically built into them. Consider, on the other hand, the march of civilisation, surely an uncontroversial process. When I say it is rapid I might mean a number of things, for example that some society is rapidly becoming more civilised, or that the area that is civilised is becoming larger, or both. In other words, several

---

[16] This is, on the other hand, denied by four-dimensionalists, who take a persisting entity to be, by definition, extended in time.

dimensions of a process might be rapid, and I may have to say which to attribute rapidity to it unambiguously. Just so for an organism. My claim is that we cannot avoid a concept of continuant process (e.g. rivers, vortices) and given that we have one it is by far the most apt for describing living systems. Moreover, if the need for such a concept is admitted there must be something amiss with a conceptual framework that rules it out a priori.

A final thought here is that perhaps what is ultimately at stake is whether metaphysics or empirical science comes first. Put another way, is our metaphysics naturalistic or a priori? The difference is nicely illustrated by Wiggins's remarks on the beginnings of human life:

> Suppose ... that ... we began with ... the conception of human being; and suppose that, as it stood, this conception allowed us to think of a human being as starting its existence as a zygote. The trouble would be that, as is well known, the human zygote may divide at any moment before the twelfth day after conception and give rise to two separate embryos (twins). It follows that the principle corresponding to the conception of human beings that we began with cannot stand. It is a mistake to think of a human being's existence as starting before the formation of the embryo (2016, 276).

The argument is clear enough. Logic dictates that a thing cannot be identical to two things that are not identical to one another. But from a biological point of view, it seems to me, the notion that the beginning of human life is determined by the (usually unrealised) possibility of fission seems bizarre; as, indeed, does the idea that the zygote is not part of (the life cycle of) a human being. The obvious inference is that there is something wrong with the conceptual framework that leads to such a bizarre conclusion.

How would we describe this situation from a process perspective? The whole apparatus of being the same thing, totally present at all times that it exists, has no application. A living process begins to emerge from another at a moment initiated by the fertilisation of an egg.[17] This process may divide into two during its earlier stages. Are the developing homozygotic twins parts of the same process? Yes, in exactly the same sense that the Mississippi and the Missouri are parts of the same river system. No, in the sense that we may define the Mississippi in a way that excludes the Missouri, and this may come to have important social consequences. For many reasons, we are much more likely to adopt an analogue of the second conceptual division in the human case. We have many reasons for distinguishing individual human lives as identifiable processes. But there is nothing mysterious happening here, as when our

---

[17] This process has come under philosophical scrutiny in recent work on the metaphysics of pregnancy. See Kingma (2019), and with an explicitly processual perspective, Meincke (forthcoming).

philosophical commitments force us to hypothesise the coming into being of an individual due to the expiration of a fairly small probability of twinning.[18]

5 Biological Kinds

It has often been assumed that the existence of things of certain kinds is among the basic facts about the world, and that one of the aims of science is to distinguish and describe such kinds. Since the nineteenth century, and the work of philosophers such as William Whewell and John Stuart Mill, this view has been associated with a doctrine of natural kinds.[19] While it is obvious that some kinds are not natural in the relevant sense – we don't need scientists to discover pencils or honorary professors – others, such as platinum, platypuses and pulsars are often thought of in this way. They are *natural* kinds, kinds that existed as such long before anyone discovered them or their characteristics. In the philosophical tradition from Aristotle onwards, some of the most commonly proposed examples of such naturally occurring kinds have been biological species, and perhaps taxa at higher levels, such as genera, families, etc. This section will consider the status of such biological classifications.[20]

I noted in the last section the role of essences in determining the identity over time of a thing, and here I note the other, probably more familiar, role of essences, as determining the kind to which a thing belongs. It is an attractive feature of the traditional thing-centred metaphysics that these roles should coincide. A cow, one might naturally suppose, exists for as long as it remains a cow. A cow could not change into a different cow, nor could it change, somehow, into a horse or a cabbage,[21] and remain the same thing. Both these last propositions can be challenged, but they are certainly natural and plausible

---

[18] The different perspectives of philosophers of biology and metaphysicians on questions such as individuality and identity over time have frequently resulted in a complete and regrettable absence of communication. Anne Sophie Meincke and I have attempted to initiate a dialogue in (Meincke and Dupré 2020). See also (Guay and Pradeu 2015a) which also includes perspectives from physics. See Meincke (2020) for detailed arguments for the claims of the preceding two paragraphs.

[19] The history of the idea, and a compelling argument that it is no longer of any philosophical interest, are outlined by Ian Hacking (2007). Ironically, he also notes, natural (or, in Whewell and Mill, 'real') kinds originated in the nineteenth century as a strongly anti-essentialist doctrine.

[20] In this section, I focus exclusively on taxonomic kinds, as is standard practice in discussions of biological kinds. As an anonymous referee pointed out, there are other candidates in biology. Some of these are clearly functional (predator, heart, etc.) and no one would expect these to be materially, or structurally homogeneous. DNA, polypeptide and the like are kinds of chemistry, which puts them outside the scope of this discussion. I suspect that other candidates would be amenable to similar arguments to those developed below. Finally, I have argued before (Dupré 1993) that many biological kind names refer to respectable but non-scientific kinds. In a book on the metaphysics of biological science, however, these can safely be ignored.

[21] Fairy tales in which princes turn into frogs and vice versa, or humans turn into beetles, inevitably assume a kind of mind/body dualism that most philosophers would now firmly reject.

assumptions. If the cow has an essential property, and essences serve both the roles just distinguished, this entails that it will both continue to exist and remain the same cow for just as long as it continues to possess the relevant essential property.

The problem, as I have already mentioned, is that there do not appear to be any suitable properties in biology to serve as essences. From antiquity, essences have generally been taken to be normal observable properties – colour, shape, number of appendages – so-called morphology. More recently, in keeping with a commonly alleged general scientific tendency to look for hidden, microscopic causes, the relevant properties have often been assumed to be genetic. Biological experts on classification, on the other hand, taxonomists and systematists, impressed by the power and importance of evolutionary thinking, have increasingly considered ancestry to be the decisive basis for membership of a kind, and therefore as providing, if anything does, the essential properties of biological kinds. Unfortunately, as I shall now explain, none of these proposals can do the work required of it.

Beginning with morphology, the possibility of morphological essences was dealt a final and fatal blow by the theory of evolution. Evolution by natural selection requires that species exhibit variability, and this is in fact the case. There is no particular limit on the extent of variability. There are, of course, limits on variability set by viability and, more subtly, by the degree of integration into the overall functioning of the organism. All humans have a heart and a liver, since without these they could not survive;[22] and no humans have six limbs, because there is just no viable developmental pathway that leads from a human embryo to a viable hexapodal organism. The problem with such putative essential properties is that they certainly cannot distinguish a human from a host of other organisms. A human essence must be possessed by all humans and no non-human apes. It is highly plausible that any property that characterised every chimpanzee could in principle be acquired by a human.

There are other simpler problems for morphological essentialism. Males and females of the same species can sometimes diverge dramatically in morphology. One striking example occurs in a genus of moths that mimic other species, but in which the sexes mimic different species (Moraes et al. 2017). The females of the two species *Dysschema maginata* and *D. terminata* actually share the same wing patterns, while the males not only differ from these, but in the case of the latter species the males exhibit at least four distinct phenotypes. Unsurprisingly,

---

[22] This is not strictly true, as even physiologically defective humans who must die very shortly after birth are human while still alive. This is a complication that only exacerbates the problems for essentialism.

the classification of these insects was very difficult before the introduction of DNA-based methods.

Still more serious is the problem of metamorphosis in development. Can an egg, a tadpole and a frog, or egg, larva, pupa, and adult insect, really instantiate the same morphological essence? I shall return to this issue in the next section in the context of reasons for thinking of organisms as processes, but for now it provides one more nail in the coffin of the idea of gross morphology as filling the role of essence.

The preceding problems are likely to encourage the thought that there might be a hidden, internal, probably genetic essence, an idea that became popular with the rise of molecular genetics in the 1960s and 70s, and became philosophically notorious through examples used by Saul Kripke and Hilary Putnam (e.g. Putnam (1975), p. 240). But it soon became clear that this suggestion escapes few of the problems raised by macroscopic morphology: the genetic structure of members of a species is just as variable as their morphology. Genetic features that are central to the proper development of the organism will likely be shared with many other related organisms; and there is no reason to expect genetic features sufficiently marginal to differentiate the organism from related kinds to be possessed by every member of the species.[23]

An evolutionary perspective not only raises problems for these traditional modes of essentialism, but it also suggests a quite different approach. Kinds, from an evolutionary perspective, should be thought of as connected by relations of common descent rather than by common possession of any property. This perspective explains the dominant cladistic account of biological taxa: a taxon is a part of the phylogenetic tree.[24] Or so it has very widely been argued. In fact, when I said that evolution assumes variation within a kind I was covertly assuming that kinds formed the parts of the lineages within which evolution takes place. But what makes organisms parts of the same lineage is common ancestry, and there is no reason, a priori or empirical, why organisms sharing ancestors should have the same morphological or genetic properties.

Strangely, despite compelling arguments and the almost universal consensus of philosophers of biology, essentialism in biology will not go away. The most recent attempt to revive it has been by Michael Devitt (2008; 2010). Devitt takes the essence of being an F to be the property in virtue of which something is an F (Devitt 2010, 649). Put very simply, Devitt wants to argue that species concepts are explanatory, and that to be explanatory they require intrinsic

---

[23] For more problems with genetic essentialism, see Dupré 2012, ch. 7.

[24] For cladists a taxon is a monophyletic part of the tree of life, that is, it contains all and only the descendants of some ancestral taxon. Put more metaphorically, if the tree of life were a real tree, any cut through one of its branches would lead to a monophyletic group falling off.

essences. Why is Tony striped? Devitt thinks that the answer to this is: because he is a tiger. Why are tigers striped? Because they have a certain intrinsic property, probably genetic, that makes them so. Tigers, it seems, must have the relevant internal structure that makes them tigers and must, therefore, at least under normal conditions, be striped.

I don't believe that being a tiger explains why Tony is striped. Let me allow that for all striped tigers there is an internal, causal explanation of their being striped. If being a tiger explains why Tony is striped, then this internal causal factor must be part of the intrinsic essence that Devitt supposes belongs to the kind, tiger. I can't here go in any detail into the reasons why there is such a strong consensus among philosophers of biology that there is no such essence to be part of, nor Dennett's objections to the consensus. I will make just one important but not so familiar point. The robustness of biological systems frequently depends on the possibility of features being generated by multiple different routes, part of the reason why organisms often develop quite normally despite the disabling of apparently functional genes. There is no reason why this causal redundancy should not be true of tiger stripes, and so no reason to suppose that the same explanation is true for the stripiness of all tigers. In short, while it may be a harmless feature of everyday discourse that we explain stripiness by pointing out that a creature belongs to a species most members of which have stripes, this is a poor apology for a *scientific* explanation. Devitt acknowledges that there is an almost complete consensus that essentialism in biology is false. I am proud to remain a subscriber to that consensus.[25]

Might the phylogenetic conception of species provide a quite different kind of essential property, a historical essence? It has been argued that this is the case, notably by Paul Griffiths (1999). I should first note that this is a very weak notion of essence that doesn't serve many of the functions that have traditionally been expected of essences. It will not, for instance, help with answering questions of individuality over time, as certainly no entity can change its ancestors. And Griffiths explicitly denies that this notion of essence can ground universal regularities. Phylogeny can, indeed, provide a kind of explanation of why an organism of a particular kind has a particular feature. Why does Tony have stripes? Because he belongs to a kind of animal descended from an ancestral population that was all or mainly striped, and being striped is a heritable property of those organisms. This is a feeble explanation. It certainly adds little or nothing to the generalisation that tigers are striped, and says nothing about what it is about tigers that makes them develop stripes. I also

---

[25] Much more detailed criticism of Devitt's essentialism can be found in Barker (2010), Ereshefsky (2010) and Leslie (2013). Devitt replies to these in Devitt (2021).

see no reason to bring essences in here. But the work they are asked to do is so minimal that I am not much bothered if anyone really wants to do so.

Another problem with historical essences that will be important later in this Element, is that the tree of life is a messier object than is often supposed. First, species can merge as well as split,[26] which implies that lines of ancestry may be ambiguous, though since only closely related species are in practice likely to merge this may not be a very serious problem. But second, the boundaries between species are much less clear than one might imagine. This is because hybridisation, interbreeding between members of different species, is common. Reproductive compatibility can survive a good deal of divergent evolution, and lead to a considerable amount of reticulation in the tree of life (Mallet et al. 2016). But finally, there is a lot of lateral flow of genetic material quite outside the familiar process of sexual reproduction. This lateral gene transfer (LGT) is so common in microbial life that it makes it very probably impossible to draw any unique tree for this part of the phylogenetic tree – the only part for most of the history of life (Bapteste et al. 2009). And even in macrobial life LGT can occur. Most familiarly this is through the action of retroviruses that can add genetic material to the nuclear genome of eukaryotes. A well-known example is the genes that code for the syncytium in the mammalian placenta (Lavialle et al. 2013). The upshot of all this is that identifying the set of ancestors for a particular extant species is a much more difficult project than has often been assumed. I do not think it is fertile ground for the growth of essences.

So far, this section has considered biological classification in a fairly general way, potentially to include classifications at all levels of the Linnean hierarchy, from species to kingdoms. I should mention, however, that the majority of philosophical discussion has been addressed more specifically to the species. It used to be common to claim that biological species are real, whereas higher taxa were merely human artefacts. This view has gone out of fashion mainly because it makes little sense from a phylogenetic, certainly from a cladistic, point of view. Nothing constrains a tree to have a particular number of branching levels, and neither oak trees, nor trees of life, in fact do. There is nothing that specifically distinguishes the level of the species.

There are, however, well known conceptions of the species that do differentiate it sharply from other categories, most notably the understanding of the species as a group of organisms connected to one another and isolated from other organisms by reproductive relations. Two individuals are members of the same species on this view if and only if they are connected by relations of

---

[26] Speciation by hybridisation appears to be common in plants.

potential reproduction.[27] The idea is most strongly connected with Ernst Mayr, who named it the Biological Species Concept (see, e.g., Mayr 1982, pp. 270–285). Unfortunately, though there is no doubt of the importance of reproductive relations and reproductive isolation in understanding biological diversity, as an account of species this will not work. First of all, it has no application to the vast number of biological kinds of asexual organisms. Unless we ignore prokaryotes (bacteria and archaea) the vast majority of organisms are asexual. If they are not considered to form species, then the concept of species becomes a lot less central to biology than is generally supposed. But even apart from this, hybridisation, as noted above, is far more common than is generally supposed (Mallet et al. 2016). The integrity of species, moreover, appears to be able to survive long periods of hybridisation with adjacent species, so the criterion of reproductive isolation is inapplicable.

I shall not say much more about the so-called 'species problem', the problem of what constitutes a group of organisms as a species, as this leads quite quickly into technical issues of limited philosophical interest. Mayden (1997) claimed that at least twenty-two concepts of the species were in use at the time of writing. While Mayden wished to assert the primacy of one of these, others have thought it better to accept and live with some level of plurality (Ereshefsky 1992; Dupré 1999). These so-called pluralists have argued that there is no unique way of dividing the domain of biological organisms into distinct kinds, and that different legitimate divisions serve different purposes. I have myself argued that this extends even beyond scientific purposes to the classifications of the forester or the chef (Dupré 1993, ch. 1), part of a position I refer to as 'promiscuous realism'. Most writers on the topic have wanted to limit kinds to those of interest to science. I shan't pursue this debate here beyond noting that the latter view seems likely to require a robust criterion for what is and is not science, something of which I am sceptical. But let me quickly defend the realism in promiscuous realism. In my view pluralism is grounded not on the denial that there are any naturally occurring distinctions on which to ground discrete kinds, but on the belief that there are too many, and they may overlap and cross-cut. Hence, there is nothing to prevent one from being a pluralist and a realist, from believing that there are many ways of classifying phenomena, and that many or all of them may reflect real and important divisions in nature.

I cannot leave the topic of biological species without mentioning a metaphysical topic that has been one of the most widely discussed in the philosophy of biology of the last few decades, the thesis promoted by Michael

---

[27] The details of such a view require some work to take care of pre- and post-reproductive individuals, and sterile individuals of reproductive age. The general idea, I think, is clear enough.

Ghiselin and David Hull that species are not kinds at all, but concrete individuals (Ghiselin 1974; Hull 1976). This is a natural extension of the view that species are parts of the tree of life. The tree is a very large and temporally extended entity, consisting of all the organisms that have ever lived, and a species is a small part of that entity. Generally, when it is supposed that membership of a kind depends on particular properties, it is expected that a member of the kind might, in principle, appear anywhere in space and time. But clearly this is not the case for kinds that are parts of a historical individual such as a species. If 'pig' names such a kind,[28] there is no organism, even molecule for molecule indistinguishable from my pet pig Porco, that could be a pig on another planet. And when the species *Sus domesticus* has gone extinct there can never be another member of it, even if again the molecule for molecule replica of Porco were to evolve or be assembled in the distant future. This is of course just what we expect for individuals. If Porco himself is dead, and has been buried or eaten, he cannot reappear however similar to him some future pig may be. In this respect, cladistically defined species are just like more familiar individuals.

There are obvious concerns with the species as individuals (s-a-i) thesis. Most obviously, the parts of this putative individual are not only spatially disconnected, but they may be disconnected causally and in every other way apart from shared historical origin. Can this alone be enough to make the members of the species parts of the same individual? And when does this individual come into being and go out of existence? An obvious solution is to conceive of species not as individual things, or substances, but as individual processes, as explained at the conclusion of the preceding section. Against this proposal, which I endorse, objections of the kind noted have no force. I will return to the conception of species as processes in a later section.

The dominant cladistic account of biological classification and the s-a-i thesis are closely connected. Both see biological classification as largely a matter of delineating the tree of life. The s-a-i thesis draws its intuitive plausibility from the observation that being a part of a tree lacks the generality widely assumed for a classificatory term. I have already noted some important reservations about this package of ideas, notably that for large parts of biology the whole notion of a tree of life is questionable. I would like now to note one further, rather more general, concern.

Cladistic classification is a very theory-driven approach to biological classification. And while no one worth worrying about doubts the 'theory' that

---

[28] And just to be clear, as a promiscuous realist I don't think this is the only legitimate interpretation of the word 'pig'. A butcher or a chef might find pigs on a distant planet.

biological diversity came about through evolution, as the doubts about the tree of life illustrate, there is a good deal of controversy about the details of the theory of evolution.[29] There is also a lot of much more routine development of detailed views of evolutionary history, often reflected in the reassignment of species to different genera, genera to families and so on.

This normal scientific development at both the theoretical and the local levels suggests a degree of conflict with more practical purposes that biological classification serves (Dupré 2001). Vast amounts of information about particular kinds of organisms are being collected all the time, and the storage and accessibility of this information depends on an effective and ideally stable classificatory system. The stability of the system is obviously threatened to some degree by full answerability to theoretical change. It would be absurd to try to maintain complete immutability in a scientific taxonomy, but it is important also to set the bar as high as possible for licensing taxonomic changes. Furthermore, a theory-driven classification may, on occasion, be very poorly suited to the practical aims it is intended to serve. From the latter point of view, it is important that taxa be neither too small, and thereby difficulty to apply, or too large, thereby embracing excessive diversity. For example, strict cladists will never allow anagenetic evolution, evolution within a lineage, to generate taxonomic difference. But it is clearly possible that such a restriction can generate taxa that are much larger and more diverse than is appropriate for many purposes. Given the topic of this Element, this might be a good point to note that metaphysics must not always be allowed to override pragmatics.

One final illustration of the importance of the pragmatic will conclude the first part of the Element. One purpose served by species distinctions is the measurement of biodiversity, most simply accomplished simply by counting the species represented in an area or ecosystem of interest. This is something that serves vital policy decisions. If pluralism is true, and there is a variety of ways in which biological diversity can be described, then it is of great importance that a measure of diversity that fits the aims of an application be applied. We need to ask why we care about biodiversity and what aspects of it we care about before deciding what species criterion we should use in measuring it. It may be that lineages branching into many rare but slightly divergent isolated groups should be given greater weight than very successful lineages with limited such separation. But this is not

---

[29] This is perhaps an understatement in view of how heated many of the controversies are. For discussions of many of the main areas of development in contemporary evolutionary thinking see the 2017 special issue of the journal *Interface Focus*, on 'New Trends in Evolutionary Biology: Biological, Philosophical and Social Science Perspectives' (Bateson et al. 2017). Some of these issues will be considered in the next section.

obvious, and certainly not something that should be accepted merely as an implication of a theoretically preferred species concept.

Part II Biological Perspectives

6 Evolution

No serious scientist doubts that the vast array of organisms of different kinds now inhabiting our planet came to be there through evolution.[30] It might seem odd for an Element on the *metaphysics* of biology to consider *why* there are living beings before asking *what* they are. However, evolution has been overwhelmingly the topic in biology most discussed by philosophers over recent decade; some philosophers like to quote from Theodosius Dobzhansky (1973): 'Nothing in biology makes sense except in the light of evolution'. As we have already seen, the classification of organisms is widely taken to be an exercise in mapping evolutionary history, and as I shall discuss below, some theorists believe that accessibility to evolution is the key determinant of whether some biological system counts as an individual or an organism. I am personally sceptical of taking Dobzhansky's dictum too seriously, as I suspect that a great deal of physiological research, for instance, has little direct connection with evolutionary thinking. Nonetheless, no one doubts that evolution is fundamentally important for large parts of biology and, for that matter, that it has some bearing on what kinds of beings these are that have evolved.

The most general sense of the expression 'the theory of evolution' is that the kinds of organisms that exist today came about through descent with modification. Expanding this into a theory specific enough to be of much interest requires saying something more about the two obvious questions, Descent from what? and Modification by what process?

The variety of possible answers to the first question is apparent in the views of the two most famous historical figures in the history of evolutionary thinking, Charles Darwin[31] and Jean-Baptiste Pierre Antoine de Monet, chevalier de Lamarck.[32] Lamarck believed that the simplest living forms were constantly

---

[30] Of course, I realise this view is controversial. According to a recent Gallup poll (https://news .gallup.com/poll/261680/americans-believe-creationism.aspx), 22% of US adults believe that human evolution occurred without any assistance from God, while 40% believe in divine creation. For reasons why this is not much of a live issue among scientists or philosophers see, e.g., Kitcher (1982).

[31] Darwin's classic work is, of course, *On the Origin of Species* (1859). The secondary literature is vast. For an authoritative introduction, see Ruse (2019).

[32] Lamarck's famous work is *Zoologie Philosphique* (1984/1809). For helpful exposition, see Burkhardt (2013).

generated spontaneously from non-living matter. These simple forms were then subject to a natural tendency for life to become increasingly complex, referred to as the 'power of life'. Thus, more complex forms had been evolving longer than simpler ones. Darwin on the other hand, believed that all extant life shared a common origin. As he wrote in the conclusion to *The Origin*: 'probably all the organic beings which have ever lived on this earth have descended from some one primordial form, into which life was first breathed'.[33]

Answers to the second question are rather more famous. Lamarck's name is almost universally associated with the idea of inheritance of acquired characteristics, whereas Darwin's is associated with evolution by natural selection. Whereas natural selection is so widely accepted that it is not infrequently assumed to be part of the very definition of evolution, inheritance of acquired characteristics, often referred to simply as Lamarckism, is, or was until very recently, considered a disastrous scientific heresy. The reality is, of course, rather more complicated. The inheritance of acquired characteristics, most famously illustrated by the suggestion that giraffes acquired long necks by stretching to reach higher branches of trees, and passing on their elongated spines to their descendants, was neither invented by Lamarck nor rejected by Darwin. It was a small part of Lamarck's theory, and one he took to be sufficiently well-known not to require much discussion (Burkhardt 2013). And it was an idea that became increasingly important to Darwin in successive versions of his own theory. In recent years, its taboo status has been threatened by increasing interest in cultural evolution and, especially, by growing evidence of the heritability of epigenetic changes to the genome with identifiable effects on the phenotype.[34] In the latter case, though not the former, it remains highly controversial whether there can be inheritance of specifically adaptive acquired characteristics, traits, like the hypothetical giraffe's neck, that are acquired because they are adaptive.

No one doubts that natural selection is a significant cause of evolutionary change. But exactly how significant is a widely-debated issue. Some prominent thinkers such as Richard Dawkins (1976) and Daniel Dennett (1996) take natural selection to be a force of almost limitless power. Most evolutionists are more qualified in their assessment, but the predominant view is that natural selection is the most important explanation of evolutionary change. The crucial starting point in exploring the issue is to distinguish questions about the selective process from questions about the origins of the variations between which selection chooses.

---

[33] In the 1860 ed. he added the words 'by the creator'.
[34] For a review with numerous examples, see Jablonka and Raz (2009).

Those most impressed by the power of selection typically insist that the changes that provide the material for selection are small and random. Given only (and they are massive concessions) (i) that there is a pathway to an adaptively[35] desirable phenotype, via a series of similar phenotypes each better adapted than their predecessor, and (ii) that there is a series of genetic mutations each accessible from the previous one, and mapping directly onto the series of phenotypic mutations, then that desirable phenotype should be reachable by a series of random genetic mutations. A great deal of Dawkins (1996) is devoted to arguing, notably with the famous example of the eye, that condition (i) can be met, that there is a series of small changes that can lead from no eye to the exquisite perfection of the eye of a modern mammal or cephalopod. The satisfaction of condition (ii), however remains a matter of dogma. Proponents of this simple model of evolution – selection of small, random, genetic changes – are typically strongly opposed to any 'Lamarckian' elements, that is, acquired, adaptive and heritable traits.[36]

The view of evolution just described emerged in the second half of the twentieth century from the dominant 'Modern Synthesis' of Darwinian natural selection and Mendelian particulate inheritance, and for a while was the dominant interpretation of Darwinism. More recently there has been a growing return to Darwin's own ideas in two crucial respects: first, the increasing acceptance of adaptive aspects to the production of selectable variation, and second in the acceptance of a pluralistic view of the processes driving evolutionary change. Both these movements reduce the pre-eminent importance of selection asserted in the Dawkinsian version of the Modern synthesis and in some cases reduce it to no more than, at best, a filter removing substandard individuals.

The most influential guise under which these 'Lamarckian'[37] elements have been introduced into evolutionary thinking has been through the movement in evolutionary developmental biology ('evo-devo') to see development, as adaptively shaped by interactions with the environment, as the most important source of selectable variation; most important because it is the way to understand the major changes that initiate new supraspecific taxa (see, e.g., Laland et al. (2015); Gilbert and Epel 2015; West-Eberhard 2003).

Evo-devo is part of an extremely complex set of developments in theoretical biology, sometimes grouped together under the heading of the extended

---

[35] By an 'adaptive' phenotype in this discussion I mean both well fitted to the conditions in which it lives, and disposed to leave descendants. These are not, of course, the same property, and the relations between them have been extensively discussed. This loose usage should, nonetheless, serve present purposes.

[36] One excellent though neglected critique of this view of selection is Reiss (2009).

[37] Not everyone involved in this movement would be happy with the use of this word.

evolutionary synthesis that cannot be discussed here in adequate detail. Further important aspects include the role of various channels of inheritance, especially epigenetic,[38] in evolution (Jablonka and Lamb 2014); the reciprocal relations between organism and environment, including the role of the organism in constructing the niche in which it lives (Odling-Smee et al. 2013); the constructive, self-organising properties of genomes (Shapiro 2005, 2017); the adaptive plasticity of development (West-Eberhard 2003); and the role of strictly physical forces in development (Forgacs and Newman 2005; Newman 2020).

A partly distinct development concerns the question of the structural levels at which natural selection operates, and the units that it selects between at those levels. Also in opposition to the gene-centred version of the Modern Synthesis, there is a growing consensus that selection operates at multiple levels (Okasha 2006), ranging from the nucleotide substitution to the group, species or even ecosystem. Interest in levels of selection was stimulated by the influential defence of group selection by Elliott Sober and David Sloan Wilson (1999). Much more recently there has been considerable discussion of whether holobionts, a multicellular organism plus all its symbiotic micro-organisms, might constitute a unit of selection. I will return to this issue in a later section. For now, it is important to note that there are several distinct contexts in which questions of levels and units of selection arise, and a good deal of clarity is required in deciding which is at stake (Lloyd 2020). Of particular concern in what follows will be questions about whether particular units function as interactors in evolutionary processes (in the sense of Hull (1980)) and questions about whether they are the ultimate beneficiaries of selective processes. But first we need to consider the question not of what is selected, but of what evolves.

7 Species, Populations, Lineages

This section returns to the topic of species, but now not as classificatory units but as evolutionary units. As such, I shall treat them as individual processes (see Section 5), an idea which will be explained further in due course. Organisms – still less genes – certainly do not evolve. If, say, giraffes evolve longer necks, this means that the giraffes living at time t + n have, on average, longer necks than the giraffes alive at time t. However much an individual giraffe may have stretched its neck it did not, thereby, evolve. We might informally refer to the

---

[38] By 'epigenetic' I mean any molecular bases of information transmissible to other cells apart from nucleotide sequence in the DNA. Sometimes this is limited to methylation (the attachment of a methyl group to a cytosine base) but this seems to me an unhelpful restriction. Histone modifications and microRNAs are other well-studied examples.

giraffes at time t as constituting a species, but since the giraffes at time t + n are also members of the same species this is not quite right. Better is to say that they form a *population*. Then we might think that a species is a sequence of overlapping populations.[39]

Curiously, since the concept of population is involved in the definition of important areas of biology – population genetics, population ecology, etc. – until recently it has received little philosophical attention, though there are some notable recent exceptions including Peter Godfrey Smith (2009) and Roberta Millstein (2009). Godfrey Smith considers a population to be 'a collection of particular things – that has the capacity to undergo evolution by natural selection' (2009, p. 6).[40] A collection is not itself an individual, I suppose, and here I agree with Millstein (2009) who argues that populations are individuals in the sense argued by Ghiselin and Hull for species, though I interpret both as individual *processes*.[41] They are composed of groups of conspecifics, and specifically 'the population is the largest number of organisms that are causally interconnected' (Millstein 2009, p. 271). A population qua individual is extended in time, so a population can evolve as the distribution of properties among its members changes. If populations and species are both individuals, a population may either be a species, or it may be part of a species

Here I shall focus on a wider concept that subsumes both the population and the species, the lineage. By a lineage, I mean any ancestral/descendent sequence of populations or species. Species and populations as individuals, then, are parts of lineages, either temporal, spatial, or both. A lineage should be distinguished from a clade. There is some unclarity in actual usage as to whether a clade is the set of individuals at a time derived from a common ancestral population, or rather the whole branch of the tree, including the ancestral population and all its descendents. Either way, most clades are not plausibly seen as individual entities. Mammalia, for example, and very likely life on Earth, are clades. But the diffuse character of interactions between the extant organisms within such large clades makes it implausible to treat them as individuals that could act in any kind of coherent way.

Lineages, on the other hand are much more circumscribed entities. The human lineage includes the ancestral population that founded Mammalia, but thereafter, at every division in the mammalian tree only one branch carries on in

---

[39] This still isn't quite right because the species at a time may consist of several populations. The rabbits in Britain and the rabbits in Australia belong to the same species but different populations. Several populations may also be said to form a *metapopulation*. I shall not pursue these subtleties here.

[40] A *Darwinian* population, his particular interest, has properties of heritable variation in fitness that explain the capacity to evolve

[41] In personal communication, Godfrey Smith agrees that a population is some kind of individual.

the direction that will eventually lead to humans.[42] All other branches are not part of the lineage. The members of a lineage extended further in time than a species are not a taxonomic unit of any kind (except in the special case of a monospecific genus, and then potentially a monogeneric family, etc.). They are, however, the streams down which evolutionary change flows, and parts of them are species and populations, at least qua individuals.[43]

I noted in an earlier section that many standard objections to the species as individuals thesis dissolve if we realise that these are individual processes rather than individual things. Consider the lineage just mentioned, that leads from the common ancestor of all mammals, believed to be a small, egg-laying, mouse-sized creature, to modern humans. The lineage at any time constitutes a species (or population), but what species it constitutes changes at some (or all, for a cladist) of the points at which the lineage branches. The degree of change within the lineage may not be sufficient to rule out its being a thing or substance if, with Wiggins, we hold that the life cycle of an organism can be part of its essential nature. But for the lineage an even more serious worry is the multiplicity of entities that can be distinguished within the flow of evolutionary change. The chimpanzee lineage, for example, is the same as the human lineage for the vast majority of its history, but distinct for the final few million years. Every species has a lineage partly distinct from every other, but any two species have lineages that are identical for some portion of their histories. There are at least as many lineages as there are species.

Consider and compare, once again, my favourite river example. The Mississippi as actually denoted by that name seems to me a perfectly respectable individual. What defines the upper Mississippi rather than the Missouri as part of it? In part, of course, convention as it could surely have been decided the other way. But given the decision that has been made, there is a criterion: the Mississippi comprises the flow of water from its source in Lake Itasca, Minnesota to the Gulf of Mexico. The Missouri, apart from any vagueness at its confluence with the Mississippi, does not partake in such a flow, though after the confluence it joins and mingles with it. So to be part of the Mississippi is to be part of an activity. This is, of course, exactly what it is to be part of a process. When your path down the street is overtaken by a riot you are not part of the riot unless you decide to start rioting. To be part of a thing, on the other hand, is to be located within a reasonably determinate boundary. One might suppose that the

---

[42] I ignore the minor complication of hybridisation subsequent to species division, for example between *Homo sapiens* and Neanderthals and Denisovans. By definition, since speciation is assumed to have occurred, this does not obscure the major outlines of the lineage.

[43] As discussed in an earlier section, the pluralism I advocate holds that 'species' as a classificatory term may apply to many kinds of kinds that are not evolutionary units.

whole Mississippi river system was a thing, bounded by a very long continuous riverbank. But if this were a very large and curiously shaped swimming pool it would not be a river, because rivers flow. The Mississippi alone is a process rather than a thing both because to be a river is to be doing something, and also because a more particular activity defines a subpart of the overall process exhibited by the river system. The combination of the Missouri and the lower Mississippi is a similar process that just happens not to have been given a name. The Missouri alone is the flow of water from the confluence of the Jefferson and Madison rivers in Missouri Headwaters State Park, Montana,[44] to its merger with the Mississippi. Ontologically it is a rather strange part of the flow to name, pointing again to the fact that such names often reflect human interests rather than ontological boundaries.

It should be admitted that the phylogenetic tree differs from a river in being a (predominantly) divergent rather than convergent process, and that where rivers are defined by their source, lineages are defined by their destinations. Nonetheless in both cases it is participation in an activity that determines what is comprised by the individual, and any number of individuals can be parts of the overall process.

To sum up, lineages are the evolutionary processes that lead to species. Populations are spatial or temporal parts of species, up to and including, in some cases, the full spatial and temporal extent of the species. Any such temporary divisions are fairly arbitrary. Spatial divisions can be defined by more or less complete lack of interaction between distinct populations. Species, then, are the terminal twigs of the divergent tree-like evolutionary flow. But strictly speaking the terminal twigs are individual organisms. So how are species demarcated? We cannot, of course, say that species are the groups resulting from the last branching event, since branching event is a synonym for speciation, immediately leading to circularity.

One traditional answer to the last question we have already encountered is reproductive isolation. If every organism existing at a time were a member of exactly one reproductively connected group, reproductively isolated from every other organism, this would provide an exact sorting of organism into species. But as we have seen, asexual organisms and hybridisation make this criterion of very limited usefulness. The reality is messier. Mapped onto a multidimensional quality space we will find some sharply defined clusters of organisms, often connected by exclusive reproductive links, and other areas where the transitions between kinds are much more continuous. Corresponding to these morphological gradients will be levels of interaction, notably reproductive relations

---

[44] According to Wikipedia, Missouri River, accessed 9 January 2021.

construed as broadly as possible. Social cooperation that facilitates reproductive success would be included under this broad umbrella.

Vertebrate animals come reasonably close to the ideal of reproductive isolation. Hybridisation may be quite common, but does not necessarily break down barriers to gene flow. At the other extreme one might think of bacteria. Among bacteria there are no sexual links, but there is a good deal of horizontal gene transfer. This transfer should more strictly be divided into two categories, homologous recombination, between particular parts of the genomes of closely related bacterial strains, and horizontal gene transfer between sometimes very distantly related organisms.[45] It is sometimes argued that where homologous recombination occurs with a high frequency there may be genuinely species-like entities where this recombination maintains the coherence of the taxon over time. It is also possible that a set of interconnected selective forces will maintain a precise phenotype from which small deviations will be uniformly less fit. This could be described as a situation in which the conditions of existence were sharply clustered. It is reasonable enough to call these, also, species, though it should be recognised that the processes that maintain them as such are quite different from the more familiar one of reproduction with gene exchange. But there is no reason at all to assume that either of these situations will apply across the microbial world, and there may be areas of microbial diversity in which continuous change can be observed across multiple dimensions, and no multi-dimensional clustering occurs at all. In this case, it may be necessary to impose some kind of ultimately arbitrary taxonomic order, but it would be a mistake to infer from this the existence of any species in the ontological sense I have described.[46] The implication that there may often be no lineages of bacteria of the kind that generate individual processes fits with the idea that relatively frequent lateral gene transfer implies ancestry from multiple sources. Defining the lineage of a population of bacteria would be rather like tracking a single course of a river through a delta like that of the Ganges. Constant divergences and convergences of flow make this a largely arbitrary exercise.

So from this ontological perspective it seems best to see speciation as an isolation of a branch of the phylogenetic tree that happens as a matter of degree, and not at all in many wide areas of biological diversity. But if this is right it shows very clearly the importance of distinguishing species as an ontological

---

[45] See Doolittle (2019) for discussion. In one well-documented case, the thermophilic bacterium *Thermatoga maritima*, appears to have acquired a substantial proportion of its genome from Archaea, generally considered a distinct microbial kingdom (see Nelson et al. 1999).

[46] As so often, it is vital not to conflate species as taxonomic units with species as individual entities (Dupré 2001). We always need the former for practical purposes, but this does not imply the existence of the latter.

entity connected to a certain kind of evolutionary process, from species as the smallest taxonomic unit.[47] In the best cases these coincide. But in many others they don't, not least because there may not be an ontological entity of the right kind. And taxonomy must go on all the same to serve the crucial if mundane functions of storing and communicating biological information.

8 Organisms and Individuals

I have assumed so far that the constituents of species and populations, or more generally lineages, are organisms. So what is an organism? One online dictionary gives a simple answer: 'An individual animal, plant, or single-celled life form'.[48] This definition seems unexceptionable (barring a quibble about the omission of multicellular stages of fungi), but as is often the problem with definition by enumeration, it is silent on what unites these different categories under the wider heading of organisms. Wikipedia[49] has a rather different approach: 'In biology, an organism is any individual entity that embodies the properties of life. It is a synonym for "life form".' On the negative side, this seems too broad. Aren't cells, for instance, individual entities that embody the properties of life, even when they are not single-celled life forms? On the positive side, it is clear that an adequate definition will require saying something about the properties that make an entity alive. I shall defer the question of what is to be alive until the final section. For now, I will ask only what kinds of living individuals are organisms.

I must begin this discussion by noting that the terminology here has become confusing. Peter Godfrey Smith in his highly influential book *Darwinian Populations and Natural Selection* (2009) uses 'organism' in a very loose way to refer to anything that interacts in a more or less integrated way with its environment. To refer in a more specific and narrower way to a kind of entity that composes populations more or less susceptible to evolution by natural selection he uses the term 'Darwinian individual'. This has encouraged a tendency to treat 'individual' or 'biological individual' in the context of theoretical biology as referring to a subset of organisms. But this is odd: surely an organism is an individual of some kind or other? In this Element, I use the term 'individual' very broadly, and consider more specifically what constitutes individual organisms, cells, lineages, etc. I hope that this usage is clear enough,

---

[47] There are smaller units for various purposes, such as subspecies, breeds and varieties. I follow Darwin in supposing that there is no important ontological difference between a species and a subspecies, and take the general point to be, once again, that attributing taxonomic status to groups is an art as much as a science.

[48] (www.lexico.com/en/definition/organism)   [49] *Organism.* Accessed 9 January 2021.

but that the reader will not take it as reliably transferable to the work of other authors. I'll say a bit more below about Godfrey-Smith's Darwinian individuals.

Many biologists would offer an even simpler enumerative definition of an organism: organisms are single cells, such as bacteria or amoebae, or, under certain conditions, the entity composed of the descendants of a single cell.[50] The main conditions just referred to are, first, that these descendant cells form some kind of integrated whole and, second, that the cells forming this whole are to some extent functionally and morphologically differentiated. Absent this second condition we have a colony, or a congregation, but not an organism. A more controversial further condition is that the originating cell is part of a segregated germline; only specialised reproductive cells in the integrated whole go on to produce further multicellular organisms. Focusing for now on just the first two conditions, we have a conception that I have in the past referred to as a monogenomic differentiated cell line (or MDCL). The cells are (almost) genomically homogeneous because they are a few generations away from the same ancestor. So organisms are either single cells or MDCLs. Cells, conversely, are either organisms, or parts of MDCLs. None of the simple accounts of the organism I have considered so far explains what distinguishes an organism from other individuals that embody the properties of life. In an attempt to address this question, I shall consider the two disjuncts of this last definition of the organism in turn. But first I need to say a bit more about the general concept of a biological individual.[51]

Biological individual is a broader category than organism. My liver, a cell in my liver, or a pride of lions are biological and are individuals. By their being individuals I mean at least that there is some integration of their parts and some differentiation from other entities that are not parts of them. So the mereological sum of my nose and my sister's cat do not constitute an individual. More than merely integration, an individual should be expected to do something, to interact as a whole with other parts of the world. The contents of my desk drawer though they may be roughly integrated – the drawer is very full – and separated from other things – by the structure of my desk – do not do anything as a unit.

In a recent talk, Samir Okasha (2020) has questioned the general practice of talking about biological individuals, on the grounds that 'individual' is what J. L. Austin called a substantive hungry term. It requires more specification, as

---

[50] There is a much-discussed complication here deriving from the possibility of vegetative reproduction, as through strawberry runners or iris rhizomes. When, if ever, is growth reproduction? Many biologists bite the bullet here and say never, concluding that the strawberry plants derived from runners are parts of the mother plant not new individuals.

[51] For a more detailed discussion, see Wilson and Barker (2019).

in individual person, or individual tree. I think this is a useful warning. Here, by 'biological individual' I mean individual x, where x is one of a large class of biological kinds. In what follows, I shall look for conditions that a biological kind referred to by a substantive should satisfy to be a suitable qualifier of 'individual'.

None of the above is very restrictive. Okasha's point cautions us to be careful to specify what kind of individual we are talking about, but leaves open the possibility that there are a great many different kinds of individuals. In my view, there is a subjective, anthropocentric aspect to being an individual, and hence I don't believe that the question how many biological individuals there really, objectively are makes sense. Consider a lichen. This consists of a fungus (a multicellular organism) and a very large number of photosynthetic bacteria. Presumably all of these, the fungus, all of the bacteria, and the lichen itself are individuals. What about the population of bacteria? Or subpopulations with a particular mutation? Or what about the lichen-covered tree of which this particular lichen is part? There surely could be reasons for distinguishing any of these individuals, and ways in which the entities composing them could be integrated and differentiated from other entities that could ground such distinction. This is a position I have called 'promiscuous individualism' (Dupré 2012). Just as for my promiscuous realism about kinds, the point is not that there are no boundaries suitable for delineating individuals, but that there are too many. Which we choose to recognise depends on our reasons for recognition. But one may reasonably hope that the concept of organism provides a more sharply defined subset of the set of all possible biological individuals.

All individuals, I have said, do, or are at least capable of doing, something. So organisms, I suppose, are distinguished among biological individuals by what they do. What do they do that is distinctive? A tempting answer is that they reproduce. Of course, the cells inside a multicellular organism reproduce but a crucial difference relates back to the segregation of the germline mentioned above. While cells in my liver can reproduce, their ability to do so is temporally limited. When I die, so will they. My reproducing has come to an end a fair time before that of my liver cells; and whereas my liver will end when I do, my lineage may continue much longer. So a definition of organism that motivates the inclusion of just microbes and MDCLs is that they are the reproducing elements of potentially indefinite lineages.

I think this is quite substantially correct, but there is a fly or two in the ointment, of which the most troublesome is symbiosis. Consider first microbes. Microbes, single-celled organisms, are by far the most numerous organisms on the planet whatever else may count as an organism. There are estimated to be of the order of 10^{30} bacteria on Earth, and large numbers of archaea and eukaryotic single-celled organisms, such as protists and algae.[52] If one thinks of a microbe as an autonomous, independent, dividing cell, which, by virtue of its capacity to divide provides the material for a lineage extending indefinitely into the future, then it perfectly fits the account of an organism.

The trouble is that microbes are not typically independent and autonomous. Vast numbers of them live in symbiotic relations with multicellular organisms, a point to which I shall return shortly. But even microbes with no relation to a macrobe[53] are not typically independent agents. Bacteria exist in two life styles, independent, floating freely, generally in liquids, referred to as 'planktonic', and sessile, in social structures known as biofilms (Donlan 2002). It appears that the latter is the state in which most bacteria spend most time, and even planktonic bacteria may often be in transition between biofilms.

Biofilms may involve a single strain of bacteria, but most frequently involve many different kinds, organised around a sometimes complex division of labour (Elias and Banin 2012). Tasks include, in addition to distinct stages in the metabolism of the resources on which the constituents of the biofilm subsist, adhesion to the surface on which the biofilm resides and production of the ingredients of the extracellular matrix, a film which protects the bacterial cells from various external threats, including to a variable extent animal immune systems. Complex biofilms typically have a quite specific life cycle, with a sequence of colonisations, a mature condition, and a dispersal phase.

There has been a good deal of debate recently about the ontological status of biofilms. Ereshefsky and Pedroso (2013) argue that biofilms are biological individuals. Given the points just noted this seems clearly to be the case given my broad usage of 'individual'. But what kind of individual are they? Ereshefsky and Pedroso draw on David Hull's well-known distinction between interactors and replicators and argue that biofilms are interactors. They engage, as a whole, with their biotic and abiotic environment. They are not replicators, however. New biofilms may be formed that are very similar to an existing one. But it is likely that the later biofilm will be assembled from cells that originated in many different earlier biofilms. There is no biofilm that is the unique parent of a biofilm.

This all seems fine. Ereshefsky and Pedroso, however, seem to suggest that their analysis helps to answer the question of what a biological individual is. They think that the case of biofilms favour Hull's account of biological

---

[52] There are also probably ten times this number of virus particles. Most biologists do not count these as living, though I am sceptical of the grounds for this (Dupré and Güttinger 2016; Dupré and O'Malley 2009).

[53] I refer to multicellular organisms as macrobes (O'Malley and Dupré 2007). But note that these are not the same as MDCLs as will become clear soon.

individuals as being interactors. They also argue that the case of biofilms is problematic for Godfrey-Smith's (2009) highly influential account of Darwinian individuals as whatever entities compose populations more or less susceptible to evolution by natural selection. But for the reason given by Okasha, I think this is a bad question. Ereshefsky and Pedroso show convincingly that biofilms are interactors, but are they perhaps also Darwinian individuals?

Godfrey-Smith (2009) is interested in individuals that are participants in processes of evolution by natural selection. He argues that there are three factors that create such a capacity, and that the different degrees to which the members of a population exhibit these define different degrees to which they are Darwinian individuals. These factors, reproductive bottlenecks, such as the single cell zygote stage in sexual reproduction, parent-offspring relations, and reproductive division of labour are almost entirely absent in biofilms. The paradigm for such an individual, and hence of the kind of individual that can form the kind of Darwinian population that Godfrey-Smith aims to characterise, is an MDCL with sexual reproduction and segregated germline, a human, for example. But again, the fly in the ointment is that such MDCLs actually occur only, or almost only, in complex symbiotic relations with other organisms, mainly microbes.

If we think of life as the set of all terrestrial cells, the vast majority of these occur in two kinds of aggregation, communities of microbes, such as biofilms,[54] and multicellular organisms, including their associated microbes. The latter have come to be generally known as holobionts. What kinds of individual are these multispecies communities?

We have seen compelling reasons to believe that biofilms are integrated individuals and Hullian interactors. All cells in a biofilm benefit from the shared extracellular matrix and metabolic processes are distributed among distinct cell types. In addition, and of considerable potential significance, the physical organisation of a biofilm allows high levels of lateral gene transfer. This allows for the sharing of genetic resources, such as antibiotic resistance, between cells in the community.

Holobionts, consisting of an MDCL and all associated microbes, seem even more clearly an integrated individual and an interactor. Holobionts, not MDCLs, are what we encounter as other humans and other organisms as we go about our lives. Whereas we might once have supposed that a human was an MDCL, the increasing realisation of the dependence of the whole on microbial

---

[54] Henceforward, to simplify discussion I shall allow biofilms to stand in for all kinds of integrated and differentiated microbial communities. The questions with which I am here concerned apply mainly to multispecies individuals.

symbionts for a wide range of essential functions including at least digestion, development, and the immune system, makes this assumption indefensible. It is true that seeing the human as interactor as a holobiont rather than an MDCL introduces a serious element of vagueness, as the extent to which different associated microbes serve necessary functions for the whole is highly variable. But this, I suggest, is just how the facts have turned out: the boundary between a biological individual and its environment is not a sharp one.

Given the promiscuous individualism I have already endorsed I have no objection in principle to the possibility that holobionts and biofilms are inter-actors, while MDCLs and individual microbes are units of selection. Still, it is worth asking whether the former kinds may in fact be capable of occupying both roles, as is increasingly widely argued and debated (Roughgarden et al. 2018; Doolittle and Booth 2017; Doolittle and Inkpen 2018; Lloyd 2017; Suárez 2018; but see Moran and Sloan 2015; O'Malley 2017). I shall next consider the question whether multispecies individuals can be units of selection and then, recalling my claim that evolution occurs within lineages, ask whether such individuals can form lineages. If the answer to the last question is affirmative, we should conclude that multispecies individuals may, indeed, be Darwinian individuals.

A standard view on the first question goes something like this. Of course a holobiont can be selected in the sense that it does well or badly. If it dies, so, generally, do all its constituent parts. A successful biofilm may continue to send out many new colonising cells as long as it exists. But such colonising cells will not be expected to form new biofilms with descendants from the same parent biofilm. So, it seems, the biofilm has no descendants and cannot, therefore, be a unit of selection in an evolving process. There have been a range of more or less related counterarguments to this, but here I shall focus on an ambitious idea proposed by Ford Doolittle and associates in the form of a metaphor.[55]

The metaphor appears in the title of his 2017 paper with Austin Booth, where Doolittle proposes that we focus not on the singers but the song. The singers are the collaborators in a multispecies symbiosis, the song that they collaborate in producing. The song is popular (selected) and hence the individuals equipped to contribute to singing it do well too. But the individual success is a by-product of the success of the collaboration, not vice versa. There is a striking similarity here to one of the more memorable metaphors in Richard Dawkins (1976, pp. 40–41), concerning the various rowers in a crew. Dawkins imagines the

---

[55] An interesting alternative is to think of the holobiont in terms of a set of stable traits (Suárez 2020). In some ways, this conception fits better with the argument below defending holobionts as lineage forming. In this brief discussion I shall focus on Doolittle's account, as this has to date been more thoroughly developed and discussed.

difficulty of selecting the best rowers for a team given that any particular trial will depend on the skills of all eight rowers and therefore that the contribution of an individual will be impossible to measure. Suppose, then, that the coach shuffles the rowers randomly (subject to their specialised positions in the boat) over a period of time. Eventually it will emerge that particular rowers tend to be found more often in the winning boat. Even if one of their skills is cooperating in the rowing of the boat, this skill will be fully transferable to any other boat, and it is the rower, together with their cooperative tendencies, that will be selected.

Despite superficial appearances, there are crucial differences between these metaphors. Most importantly, in Dawkins's picture there is a very specific set of candidates among whom the selection takes place (in the actual example, rowers at Oxford or Cambridge). A central point about the singers and the song is that this is not the case. A song can be transposed from having a soprano solo to an alto, or a viola da gamba obligato played on a cello, while still remaining clearly the same song. The air on the G string, derived from a movement of an orchestral suite by J. S. Bach, has been played by a jazz trio (Jacques Loussier), unaccompanied voices (the Swingle Singers), or with the violin replaced by a saxophone. Doolittle and Booth (2017) argue that the unit of selection is not the entity, the holobiont, but an abstract pattern of interactions, a set of functions that contributes to the overall well-being of the holobiont or biofilm.

Can an abstract pattern really be a unit of selection? A plausible answer to this is that it can if, but only if, it can be used to define a lineage, which is a real pattern in the flow of biological activity. One kind of such pattern is the traditional species, an individual process as described in the previous section. What could be the realisation of a process consisting of abstract relations of functions? Presumably in the case of holobionts the answer is just the constant reconstruction of similar holobionts. Crucially, though, I say reconstruction rather than reproduction since the animal, say, reproduces qua MDCL, but reconstructs the functional holobiont by recruiting symbionts from the environment.

Godfrey-Smith (2015) contrasts reproduction with reconstruction as different explanations of recurring structure. The MDCL reproduces, whereas the holobiont is reconstructed. But given that successful reproduction always in fact results in a holobiont, there is a strong case for adopting a broader conception of reproduction. One natural move would be to see the recruitment of symbionts as just part of development, an input like food, required to reach a healthy adult outcome. The trouble with this is that it assumes an asymmetric focus on the eukaryote 'host', and it would surely be desirable to have an account that accommodated symbiotic associations that lack such a focal host, like biofilms.

It is not obvious why size should be a decisive feature in designating one symbiont as the recruiter and the other as the recruit.

Another reason to favour the symmetrical treatment of the partners in a symbiotic system is that it opens up the possibility of seeing a recurrence of reconstructions as an objective process in an ecological context. A slippery rock in a flowing stream, and populations of bacteria with a range of relevant capacities and dispositions make the formation of a biofilm highly likely. The recurrence of such reconstructions could certainly count as an objective process. Many processes consist of a series of discrete events made probable by a set of background conditions. Consider, for example, inflation. An imbalance between demand and supply constantly induces events of prices being increased. And the process certainly has a wide range of effects.

Our interest in deciding whether the constant recurrence of biofilms might constitute a lineage derives from whether it is a process within which evolution can occur, so we might as well treat this as a defining feature. Could a sequence of biofilms evolve by natural selection? Assume that a set of environmental and organismal capacities continue to generate biofilms with a very similar structure in similar surroundings. As already noted, the similarity need not extend to the constituent members belonging to a particular phylogenetic taxon. A microbe playing a particular role in the system, say producing an element of the extracellular matrix, mutates to provide a matrix constituent that repels grazing protists. The biofilm does better, the number of mutants increases as therefore does the probability that they will be recruited by other biofilms of the same kind. The mutant bacteria are fitter because the biofilms in which they live are fitter, and vice versa. The reproductive lineage of microbes and the reconstructive lineage of biofilms both become fitter. The microbes may benefit from the ability to contribute to other kinds of biofilms and the biofilms are engaged with selective processes involving constituents with quite different capacities, so these are quite independent processes.

I am inclined to conclude, therefore, that biofilms and holobionts as well as MDCLs and microbes may all be lineage forming entities. The idea that the former two are lineages defined by abstract sets of relations may sound strange. But it is good to remember that in another sense the most abstract entity here is the MDCL. The world is populated by holobionts and biofilms and some independent microbes. But MDCLs are like vascular systems. They are there alright, but they are almost always found intimately connected with much else. Sufficiently powerful antibiotics might perhaps isolate an MDCL as a sufficiently skilled surgeon might isolate (most of) a vascular system. In either case, it is unlikely that any such living system would survive for long in isolation.

Returning then to individuals, the preceding analysis confirms the thesis of promiscuous individualism. Because an MDCL is part of a lineage that can evolve independently from the other constituents of the holobiont in which it lives, for theoretical purposes, at least, it should be recognised as an individual. But the holobiont, the entity encountered in interaction with its wider environment, deserves similar recognition not only because of its status as an interactor but also because it, too, may be lineage forming. Recognition of the holobiont as a respectable biological individual forces us to acknowledge that the boundaries of an individual can be vague or blurred. There is no sharp criterion for which microbes are part of the holobiont, and which are merely transitory passengers. This may present philosophical difficulties for a view of the individual as a substance or thing, but offers none to the process view of the biological individual to which I now turn.

So far I have been especially concerned with biological individuals as constituents of lineages. In this final part of the section I look at the ontological status of the individual itself, and explain why an organism should not, as has generally been supposed, be understood as a kind of substance or thing, but rather as a kind of process.

Beginning with the MDCL, its status as a process should be fairly evident. Derivation from an originating cell is, after all, intrinsically dynamic and necessarily occupies an extended period of time. It might be possible to understand the organism as MDCL as the set of cells that arise at the conclusion of a process of cell divisions, but obviously this is not what is intended. First, the earlier stages of development are parts of the same individual as the later stages. The MDCL is a *developmental* process, and its character at different stages may be wildly different. What makes an egg, a caterpillar, a pupa and a butterfly stages in the career of a single organism are the causal links connecting the stages, not any intrinsic property they share in common.[56] And second, there is no suitable conclusion. There may be a final state, death, but while the organism is alive there is still cell division and retiring of old cells. No one supposes that the only real organism is a dead organism.

This last observation leads to a more general point, that I take to be a definitive condition of being a process, that its persistence requires activity. Cell division and cell death are a small aspect of this, which is most generally considered under the category of metabolism. There are trillions of events

---

[56] A natural thought, especially given the M, for 'monogenomic', in the acronym, is that the common characteristic is a shared genome. Apart from serious technical problems, such as the implication that monozygotic twins are the same individual, this proposal fails because the assumption of genomic homogeneity is in fact a grave oversimplification. For details – and reasons why perhaps MDCL is an unfortunate choice of term – see Dupré (2010).

taking place at any moment in the body of a multicellular organism, most of which contribute to its survival. This is a thoroughly non-accidental fact about living systems. They are complex systems, far from thermal equilibrium, and they maintain their complex structures by taking energy in from the environment. An MDCL is thus also a *thermodynamic* process.

The debate whether an organism is a substance[57] or a process is rendered very difficult by the complexities and ambiguities that have developed over millennia with both the concept of a substance and the concept of an organism, and the difficulty is exacerbated by the fact that the concepts of substance and process are generally taken to be in the domain of pure metaphysics, a field which generally has very minimal interaction with philosophy of biology.[58] From a biological point of view, at any rate, the two major options for the interpretation of the multicellular organism are the MDCL and the holobiont. We have seen that the MDCL is a process, which leaves the holobiont.

In fact, the holobiont, as well as sharing the reasons for taking the MDCL to be a process, introduces a further one. As we have already seen, there is no simple criterion for deciding which microbes associated with an MDCL are part of the holobiont and which not. Some parts of the microbiome are intimately connected to the overall metabolism of the system, others are merely passing, possibly pathogenic, alien entities. Between these extremes is a spectrum of more or less useful or necessary collaborating cells. A structurally stable process is typically stabilised by interactions with its surrounding environment, so it is no surprise that it has no sharp boundary. A clear but simple example might be a hurricane: it is clearly a temporarily extended individual process, but no one expects a simple criterion for precisely which volume of air is or is not part of it. A substance, on the other hand, is generally assumed to have clear boundaries. There can be vagueness about the boundaries of a thing. Is the manufacturer's label part of the coat? Are the bathroom fittings parts of the house? But these reflect the lack of sharp and socially agreed definitions of the objects. Where a process depends for its

---

[57] For this discussion I use the term from metaphysics, 'substance' rather than the more informal 'thing', as the looseness of the latter term allows inclusion of many entities, such as mountains and neighbourhoods, that may look like things but have more or less arbitrary boundaries. The exact ontological status of a mountain is an interesting question, and it may reasonably be asked whether, in a strictly philosophical sense, there really are any mountains (Smith and Mark 2003). At any rate, a mountain surely fails to meet central criteria for being a substance.

[58] Some attempt has been made to bridge the gap with the essays in Meincke and Dupré (2020), in which metaphysicians and philosophers of biology consider the status of biological (including human) individuals. The process status of organisms is defended in detail by Dupré and Nicholson (2018) and Nicholson (2018). This is criticised on behalf of a more traditional substance view by Wiggins (2016) and Austin (2020).

continued existence on interactions with its environment the boundary is necessarily blurred. When does a piece of food become part of me? The flow of material, solid, liquid and gaseous, into my body is not an accidental part of my life, but it is one that illustrates clearly the vague and changeable nature of the boundary between me and my environment.

I noted that the concept of a substance was complex and subject to long historical debate. But there are certain core ideas that recur in all or most versions of the concept. First, to understand what it is for a substance to persist is generally taken to require specifying intrinsic properties (often essential properties) that determine its existence. No such intrinsic properties define the life cycle of an organism. For a process like an organism, continuity is provided by causal links between temporal stages, not by any constant properties.

Second, the default condition of a substance is stasis. By that I mean that when a substance undergoes some change it is generally supposed that some explanation is to be expected. For a process, on the other hand, change is constant. For an abiotic process whether a thunderstorm, the erosion of a cliff, or the inflation of a currency, when the movement of air and water particles, the detachment of pieces of rock, or the changes in monetary prices end, the process no longer exists. When nothing happens inside a parrot, it is an ex-parrot. For a process, its stability, or lack of change, is often the central explanandum.

Third, a substance, is independent or autonomous. Some condition of this sort appears in all or almost all historical accounts of substance, and yet is plainly inappropriate to any living system. This is true both because of metabolism, the need of an organism to draw energy form the environment to maintain its non-equilibrium thermodynamic status, and also because of symbiosis. One of the motivations for a substance ontology is to provide an inventory of what there is. To this end, substances are countable. But as we have seen, because of the complexities of symbiosis, most organisms are not unequivocally countable. And fourth, as has been discussed earlier, substances but not processes have definite boundaries.

In sum, organisms are not the discrete, autonomous, countable, and stable elements of the living world supposed by traditional substance ontology. They are, rather, structural stabilities in a deeply intertwined and interconnected set of processes, stabilities maintained by the constant withdrawal of energy from their abiotic environment. There is no unique way of specifying and counting the individual structures, any more than one might hope to count the streams in a river delta or the raindrops in a thunder storm. Life is a process which we conceptually separate in various pragmatic ways; it is not a Noah's ark of discrete, countable, individual things.

9 Cells

The cell has been a curiously little-discussed entity in the philosophy of biology. This is curious because the theory promoted in the nineteenth century by Matthias Schleiden and Theodor Schwann, that cells are the basic units of life, and, as elaborated a bit later, that cells only arise through the division of pre-existing cells, is still widely accepted. The main division between kinds of organisms we have already noted is between single-celled and multicellular organisms. As units of life, cells were thought of as being alive and in an important sense autonomous. Hence, for cells that were part of multicellular organisms, though they contributed to the life of the organisms, they also led a life of their own.

Although cells are probably the most clearly differentiated individuals at any level of the biological hierarchy, their differentiation is not always simple. Cells are hugely diverse. Some are very large, like the egg cell of the ostrich, or the alga *Valonia ventricosa*, also known as sailor's eyeballs, a single-celled organism measuring up to several centimetres in diameter. At the other extreme, bacteria in the genus *Mycoplasma* are generally a few hundred nanometres across. The typical eukaryotic cell has one nucleus,[59] but there are also multinucleated cells, for example the multinucleated giant cells that form in inflammatory responses to some illnesses (including Covid-19) from the fusion of white blood cells (Anderson 2000). The layer of cells that forms the boundary between the mammalian placenta and fetus is a syncytium, a layer of cells fused together to form a multinucleated whole. Especially interesting, finally, are the filamentous cells, hyphae, of many fungi. Such cells may be many metres long, contain many thousands of nuclei which may be genomically diverse, and can branch and fuse with other hyphae. These raise fascinating questions about, for instance, intraorganismic competition between nuclei and the role of recombination between mycelial networks (Roper et al. 2011).

Despite the clear importance of cells, this section will be brief. This is in part simply because of the lack of discussion in the philosophy of biology with which to engage. A second reason is that unlike, say, genes and species, no one has ever questioned the reality of cells. Although the process of division may make the countability of cells a little vague, generally the existence of a cell is clear and distinct. Although there are certainly deep and difficult problems in cell biology, philosophical concerns are less obvious. But, finally, the nature of the cell will become clearer through a better understanding of the structures and molecules of which it is composed. In this section I shall look at one important

---

[59] Prokaryotic cells, bacteria and archaea, do not have proper nuclei at all.

supramolecular structure, and in the next two I shall look at some of the most important molecules.

One notable exception to the absence of philosophical literature on cell theory is Nicholson (2010). As Nicholson points out, historically the importance and implications of cell theory have been subjects of profound disagreement. The perspective Nicholson develops is of cells as belonging to a tradition of biological atomism. Emphasising the status of the cell as an autonomous living unit even in the context of a multicellular organism, he shows how cell theory has been interpreted in a reductionist way: the organism's functioning and behaviour were no more than the aggregate of the activities of its autonomous constituent cells, the true 'biological atoms', thereby implying the minimal theoretical significance of the whole organism. In this interpretation of cell theory, the cell is transformed from the fundamental unit of life to the only significant unit of life.

Unsurprisingly, this vision has been resisted by the tradition that sees life as more fundamentally realised by the organism. Nicholson identifies several criticisms of cell theory by organism-focused biologists, starting with the insistence that an organism is not a mere aggregation of cells,[60] but an individual in its own right. From the general perspective defended here, especially in the preceding section, this is surely correct. The debate over whether the organism is the holobiont or the MDCL makes little sense if both are just different aggregations of cells. If, as argued in an earlier section, downward causation is pervasive in living systems, then the claim that an organism is an individual in its own right has important consequences in that it suggests that the behaviour of cells is often a consequence of the causal powers of organisms. One important vehicle for causal influences from the whole to its cellular constituents is the sensitivity of cell behaviour, and in particular behaviour that shapes development, to physical forces that can be generated by the physical constraints on a whole tissue or even whole developing organism (Mammoto and Ingber 2010; Paluch and Heisenberg 2009).

The further substantial point that I want to make in this discussion of the cell is the sense in which a cell is not, as is often supposed, a mechanism (Nicholson 2019). There has been an enormous philosophical literature on mechanism in the last twenty years, which I cannot delve into in any detail. So I shall go back once more to the classic document in this literature, by Machamer, Darden and Craver (2000). MDC define a mechanism thus: 'Mechanisms are entities and activities organized such that they are productive of regular changes from start or set-up to finish or termination conditions'. As generally and naturally

---

[60] And, for what it is worth, intercellular fluid, bone matrix, ions, etc.

understood, this means that we have a set of things arranged in relations to one another and acting in such a way that some feature of the whole will be taken from one state to another. My objection to this picture (and, as far as I can tell, all its more sophisticated descendants[61]) is that it assumes a fixed set of entities with determinate properties, driving the system to which they contribute to its final state. But in biological systems, and cells in particular, the set of entities is not a given but a variable under constant stabilisation or alteration by the activities of the cell. The processes of which these latter are a part constitute the metabolism that maintains the whole in a state far from thermodynamic equilibrium. In my view the cell just is this process or set of processes. I shall illustrate the difference between these perspectives by looking at one important constituent of the cell, the ribosome.

The ribosome is generally described as a machine that translates messenger RNAs, transcribed from the genome, into polypeptide chains. However, I suggest that the ribosome is really more like an event or process than a machine; describing it as a machine is not merely misleading, but places it in the wrong general ontological category.

Like a great deal that happens in biology, translation of a protein comes about through the confluence of a number of entities. Central to these are the two subunits generally taken to constitute the ribosome, both of which are composed of a mixture of RNA segments and proteins. The smaller of these binds to the messenger RNA (mRNA) molecule transcribed from the genome (and subsequently processed; see Section 11) and the larger binds to the transfer RNAs (tRNAs) that carry the amino acid to be matched to a three-nucleotide codon. The two subunits bind to one another during the process of translation and then separate when the translation is complete. So a ribosome only exists as such, that is as the subunits bound together, for the length of one occasion of translation.

A further point complicates matters further. One might think that the two ribosomal subunits make up a translation machine, even if it is a single-use machine with a very limited lifespan. But it appears that the ribosome does more than just translate; it also functions as part of the quality control process for protein production. While some mRNAs are translated, others are degraded in the ribosomal event (Wu et al. 2019). As is well-known, the genetic code is redundant, several codons calling for the same amino acid, and it appears that this tendency to be degraded depends on the prevalence of particular codons. A particular tRNA recognises only a particular codon, and tRNAs are not

---

[61] A more up-to-date sense of where this topic has headed more recently can be gleaned from Glennan and Illari (2017).

equally common for all equivalent codons. A rarer tRNA will therefore slow down the translation of an mRNA with that codon. It appears, finally, that codons with rarer tRNAs increase the probability of degradation of the mRNA, perhaps because slower translation promotes degradation (Rak et al. 2018).

The point of all this is just to show that it is impossible to reduce the functioning of the ribosome even to the two subunits generally supposed to constitute the ribosomal 'machine'. What it does, that is whether it translates or degrades the mRNA it interacts with, depends on what other elements – which particular tRNAs – it is able to recruit. This reinforces the idea that we should think of the ribosomal event, the confluence of a somewhat variable collection of interacting items, rather than the ribosome as machine, a fixed structure waiting to process a specific targeted input.[62]

This example helps to articulate the picture of the cell as process, as a partly self-modifying, partly self-stabilising, but always dynamic set of functions and structures, constituting together a partially stabilised homeorhetic[63] process, the cell itself. The next two sections will further develop this picture by looking at two of the vital kinds of molecules to be found in living cells.

10 Molecules 1: Proteins

Few philosophers seriously deny that organisms are made of molecules. Putting aside questions of souls or immaterial minds, which will not concern me here, what else is there? Pedantically, one might want to note that there are sub-molecular entities, such as atoms and ions, that are important constituents of organisms, so I shall interpret 'molecule' very broadly to include these. Crucial though ions certainly are to many biological processes, it is large molecules that have especially occupied the attention of philosophers.[64]

Molecular biology has been widely perceived as a dominant theme in recent biology, especially since the famous announcement of the structure of DNA by Francis Crick and James Watson in 1953. What has emerged during that period is a reductionist position that is grounded not so much in abstract argument, as in

---

[62] For much more detail on the dynamic nature of the ribosome, see Moore (2012), who writes: 'As the field develops in these new directions, its acolytes will increasingly come to think of the ribosome as the dynamic, constantly varying structure it is and always was. As they do so, the field will move away from quasi-mechanical explanations for its properties and instead seek to understand them in terms of the particle's conformational energy landscape' (2012, p. 15).

[63] Conrad Waddington usefully distinguished homeostasis, the maintenance of a particular state, from homeorhesis, the active maintenance of a particular trajectory. So, for example, the developmental path of an organism is a classic homeorhetic process, stabilised against a wide variety of shocks and contingencies.

[64] Philosophers interested in neurobiology have paid more attention to the importance of ions.

a particular scientific perspective. This perspective focuses on just two crucial kinds of molecules in living systems, nucleic acids and proteins. Proteins are what organisms are made of, the molecules that enable both the structure and function of the organism. Nucleic acids,[65] in turn, both enable the production and assembly of the specific proteins that make up a particular kind of organism, and also orchestrate the timing of this production in a way that guides the development of the organism. This vision is grounded in Crick's notorious central dogma of molecular biology, that information in living systems flows in only one direction, from DNA to RNA to protein. Crucially, DNA is also seen as the vehicle of intergenerational inheritance, and thus this picture explains the transfer of form from parent to offspring.

It is, of course, acknowledged that there are other molecules – carbohydrates, lipids, water, the aforementioned ions – that play essential roles in the processes of life, but these are widely seen as less important or anyhow less interesting. But consider something as fundamental to life as the cell membrane. This is a massively complex structure that includes proteins, lipids, and carbohydrates, all of which play vital roles in the functioning of the membrane.[66] One crucial role of the membrane is the active regulation of the passage of all kinds of molecules (and importantly, ions) in and out of the cell. But here I shall follow the common practice of focusing on nucleic acids and proteins, which are certainly remarkable molecules. The limitations of the simple reductionist picture sketched above will also indirectly demonstrate the value of a more pluralistic understanding of the constituents of living systems. In this section I shall consider proteins, the most prominent structural and functional molecules in an organism.

Proteins consist of sequences of amino acids, and the specific sequence of amino acids is determined by sequences of nucleotides in the nuclear genome. The relationship between DNA sequence and amino acid sequence is a good deal more complicated than is sometimes supposed, and the relevant bits of DNA sequence are not typically found as a single stretch of the DNA molecule. Phenomena including the alternation of exons and introns in a coding sequence, alternative splicing, and post-transcriptional editing underlie the complexity of this relationship. These complications will not, however, be essential for the present discussion.

---

[65]   In what follows I shall talk almost exclusively of DNA. As important to the functioning of the cell is RNA, which mediates between DNA and protein. DNA is *transcribed* into RNA before being *translated* into protein, as the literary metaphor goes, and RNA is also a structural component of vital functional entities in the cell, such as the ribosome (see previous section).

[66]   Cell membranes 'reproduce' through cell division and form a lineage that goes back, presumably, to the earliest cells. That this lineage is substantially independent of the lineages of nucleic acids is surely part of the reason that it has not been much discussed.

A widely held view of the biology of proteins runs as follows. Amino acid chains fold into three dimensional structures, and this is a thermodynamic process of achieving the lowest energy state possible, perhaps with the help of a catalyst or two. The functional properties of the protein are then determined by its structure. This can be a direct connection, as with the filament forming actin and myosin central to the functioning of muscle tissue, but the widest variety of proteins function as enzymes, catalysing chemical changes within the organism.

While there is much in this picture that is still believed to be correct, the reality increasingly appears to be far more dynamic and stochastic than this rather mechanistic account suggests. Beginning with protein folding, scientific orthodoxy has moved gradually from folding as a spontaneous rearrangement of the amino acid chain, to recognition of the role of chaperones, further protein molecules that help to constrain the folding process, to the concept of proteostasis, the realisation that for many proteins maintenance of their proper structure is a lifetime task. In fact, a complex network of interacting entities including the chaperone proteins, the proteostasis network, is constantly engaged in maintaining the health of the proteome, the inventory of proteins in the cell, and defects in this network are implicated in a variety of important diseases (Balch et al. 2008). As so often in biology, what was once thought of as a set of objects interacting mechanistically with one another turns out to be a dynamic system in which the inventory of objects is itself a target variable that the system is constantly working to stabilise or adapt to varying conditions.

Turning to the functioning of enzymes, the starting point is the assumption that the enzyme binds to a target molecule, called a *substrate*, and aids its conversion to a particular *product*. The theory proposed by Emil Fischer in 1894 to explain this type of behaviour was that enzyme and substrate had precisely complementary shapes that enabled them to connect. The substrate would fit into a specifically shaped activity on the enzyme, which became known as the active site; this would change the topology or charge distribution of the substrate in a way that would lower the energy barrier to conversion to the functional product. The model is generally referred to as the lock and key model. Since Daniel Koshland's classic 1958 paper, however, it has generally been understood that the interaction between enzyme and substrate is more dynamic, and that the interaction between the two molecules reshapes both of them, an idea that has become known as the 'induced fit' model.

For some contemporary thinkers, this move towards a more dynamic view of protein function does not go far enough, however (Güttinger 2018; Stein 2004, 2006, 2020). Even with the induced fit model, the overall metaphysics remains one of an entity contingently undergoing a sequence of changes, as in the now classic model of mechanism promoted by Machamer, Darden and Carver

(2000), with its explicit grounding in a dualism of entity and activity. But modern scientific understanding of the enzyme does not see its activity as separable even in principle from the entity. First, the enzyme does not exist as a unique rigid structure prior to its encounter with the substrate, but rather as an ensemble of structures ('conformers') through which it constantly cycles, activity that is enabled by its coupling with its aqueous environment.[67] And crucially, the power to catalyse the reaction is grounded in this cycling through an ensemble of states, and on its embedding in, and dynamic relation to, its molecular environment. It is not merely a capacity of the structure of the enzyme. If activity is already an essential part of the characterisation of the entity capable of catalysis, then the entity and the activity cannot be separated in the way assumed in the dualistic mechanism of Machamer, Darden and Craver.

Moreover, the transformation of the substrate is not a simple switch from one structure to another, but involves a sequence of intermediate states. Enzyme and substrate first form a metastable unity, the substrate selecting one enzyme conformer from the available ensemble; this complex then finds the more stable, lower energy state known as the Michaelis complex; and the latter, finally, is chemically transformed into the enzyme and the product. This may still sound like a series of activities occurring to a series of things. But the more fundamental reality is that the whole inventory of enzymes and other proteins in the cell exist always as dynamic ensembles of conformers of varying stability and abundance (Stein 2020). The transformations and stabilisations of this inventory are not reducible to the activities of a set of discrete structures, but are the result of a constant negotiation between the proteins and populations of other molecules, crucially including the aqueous background. The mechanisms described in terms of entities and activities are not a more fundamental account of these population level processes, but rather simplifying abstractions therefrom.

A final observation emphasises several of the preceding points. For a long time it was common to look for the function of a protein or, conversely, to look for a protein that served an already identified function. Although this may often be a quite legitimate project, it can easily lead to the assumption that there is a one-to-one mapping of proteins to functions. However, as early as the 1980s it was known that some proteins could perform multiple tasks, and the number of

---

[67] This lack of definite structure is emphasised by the growing number of proteins that are characterised as 'intrinsically disordered', meaning that they are not considered to have any fixed three-dimensional structure. It is hard to find an agreed estimate of the prevalence of intrinsic disorder, but it is commonly supposed to happen in about one third of eukaryote proteins. It is also widely understood that intrinsically disordered proteins are specifically adapted to multifunctionality or 'moonlighting' (see below, in main text).

such cases grows steadily (Jeffery 1999, 2009). Reflecting the continued assumption that a protein has one primary job, these multitaskers have come to be known as 'moonlighting' proteins. But it seems increasingly likely that there are no such primary tasks for many or most proteins, and that the protean, shape-shifting character of the protein reflects its role as an entity suited to adapting to multiple roles rather than custom-designed for just one.

11 Molecules 2: Nucleic Acids

The most famous molecule in biochemistry is surely deoxyribonucleic acid (DNA). Erwin Schrödinger in his famous book 'What is Life?' (1944) predicted that an aperiodic crystal was likely to be the material basis of biological heredity, and the stable modular structure of DNA is perfectly suited to providing a store of information of the kind Schrödinger envisaged.[68] The question such a molecule is postulated as answering is that of how the information needed to construct an organism is passed on from parent to offspring in reproduction. Why do acorns give rise to oak trees, and pandas give birth to pandas? As is very familiar, the sequence of four nucleotides ('letters') in the DNA molecule indeed appear perfectly suited to serve this information carrying function.

This information carrying function of DNA was triumphantly confirmed not long after Crick and Watson's announcement of the structure of DNA, when it was shown that triplets of nucleotides were systematically related to the amino acids that form polypeptides or proteins. Thus, a specific sequence of nucleotides could provide the information for the assembly of an amino acid chain. I shall return to the question of the relation between DNA and proteins, but first I'll say a bit about the nature of genomes and genes.

The genome of an organism is commonly understood as the full complement of DNA in the nucleus of one of its cells – or for prokaryotes that don't have a nucleus, just the DNA in the cell. But a problem immediately arises, is the genome literally just DNA, or is it the entity, typically consisting of a number of chromosomes, that can be seen in the cell with a suitable microscope?

The genome is commonly treated as an abstract object consisting merely of a sequence of nucleotides. But the real entity observable through a microscope is much more than this. In addition to the DNA, the chromosomes include a core of proteins called histones, around which the DNA is wrapped.[69] Since the

---

[68] Schrödinger himself, however, incorrectly assumed that the hereditary material was protein. The results of Oswald Avery's famous experiments conclusively proving that DNA was the hereditary material were published in the same year as Schrödinger's book, 1944.

[69] For further discussion of these and the following points, see Barnes and Dupré 2008; Güttinger and Dupré 2016.

human genome includes DNA sequence that would measure about two metres in a straight line, and the typical cell nucleus is less than 10μm, a good deal of this wrapping, or *condensation*, is needed. Moreover, various molecules or parts of molecules attach to the threads of DNA, including the well-known methyl groups that result in methylation, an *epigenetic* modification of the DNA. If the histones were merely spools on which the nuclear DNA were stored, or the methyl groups merely clutter, fortuitously adhering to the genome, they could safely be ignored, and the identification of the genome with its DNA sequence might make good sense. But this is far from the case. Epigenetic modifications are modifications that affect the functioning of the DNA, typically by promoting or repressing expression of particular sequences. Methylation and modifications of the histones are the most studied such epigenetic changes.[70]

The first upshot of this last point is that the identification of the genome merely with nucleotide sequence is liable to encourage the erroneous supposition that the fate of the organism is derivable from its nucleotide sequence. But even more important than this is the false assumption that the genome is something fixed that carries the developmental information required to build the organism from generation to generation. The importance of recognising epigenetic changes to the genome is that these changes are contingent, often reversible, and often responsive to the environment. Contrary to the common supposition that the genome is a fixed object, containing a determinate developmental programme, it is a fluid, dynamic entity, in constant interaction with the environment.

There are purposes for which the abstract sequence view of the genome is harmless and even appropriate. Many of these concern judgements of similarities between organisms. Most notably, DNA sequence has had a profound effect on taxonomy, providing a simple and often very illuminating way of measuring the relatedness of organisms. In the same vein, it underlies technologies such as forensic genetics and paternity tracing, though in truth these generally involve only a small number of very specific features of the sequence. But for understanding evolution, development, or molecular physiology, a much richer and more realistic understanding of the genome is required.

If we think of the genome as a material thing (or, as I would personally prefer, a material process) is it composed of genes? So what is a gene? The standard answer to this question is that it is a stretch of DNA that provides the information necessary to build a single protein. One thing we can be sure of is that given any such conception, not all the genome is made of genes. Not long ago it was

---

[70] Increasing interest is developing, however, in the role of microRNAs in inheritance, both in the maternal cytoplasm and as carried by sperm cells (see, e.g., Rogers et al. 2015).

commonly said that 99% of the genome was junk, non-functional garbage that had accumulated over the long years of evolution. This estimate was based on the idea that the only thing DNA did was provide information for the construction of proteins. It is now clear at least that there are parts of the DNA that have distinct regulatory functions, and some believe that most of the genome is functional.[71] But it is at any rate clear that not all the genome consists of functional units that might qualify as genes, for example long stretches that merely repeat a short sequence of nucleotides.

Returning to the protein-coding account of what a gene is, an immediate problem is that in eukaryotes ('higher' organisms, or organisms other than bacteria and archaea) this information is provided by a sequence of segments (exons) separated by non-coding sequences (introns), and the latter are excised after the sequence has been transcribed. The sum total of the exons and introns, or more technically the sequence that comes between a start codon, a triplet that induces the transcription process to begin, and a stop codon, that makes it stop, is called an open reading frame (ORF). Is the ORF the gene, or just the set of exons?

Matters become still more complex when we look more closely at what may happen after transcription of an ORF into RNA. As the introns are removed, the exons may be assembled in a variety of different ways, sometimes thousands of ways, producing different RNA sequences and ultimately distinct proteins (*alternative splicing*). Moreover, in some of these alternative splice products exons may be deleted as well as introns. Finally, there are cases of trans-splicing, in which transcripts from different ORFs are joined together. So an ORF may provide the information for a large number of proteins, and not all parts of it need provide the information for the same set.

Given these complications, the standard conception of the gene just noted becomes highly problematic. A set of nucleotides involved in building a specific protein may be highly discontinuous even, in the case of trans-splicing, occurring on different chromosomes. And this discontinuous set may provide the sequence information for a considerable number of distinct proteins. Partially overlapping sets of sequences will provide information for different sets of proteins. Looking at the functionality of the genome, rather than trying to classify it in terms of downstream products, seems much more hopeful, which suggests, incidentally, that the ORF is a better candidate for the referent of 'gene'.

---

[71] The ENCODE project, established in 2003 to investigate the functions of elements of the human genome, was interpreted by some as showing that up to 80% of the genome was functional. Subsequently the project has encountered widespread criticism, however. For further discussion, see Güttinger and Dupré (2016).

If attempting to relate a gene to a specific RNA transcript is problematic, the idea that it may have a specific function at the phenotypic level is hopeless. So the common language of genes for height, genes for aggression, and so on, is liable to be highly misleading. This can also be seen as part of the transformation that I have advocated throughout this Element. Rather than see an array of objects with predetermined functions deployed in an order embedded in an evolved programme, we should see the genome as a fluid system, generating appropriate transcripts as determined by the responses of the system to its chemical environment, which, in turn, reflects wider features of the organism's environment, and then undergoing modifications also in response to environmental factors. The gene, then, is not a machine waiting to be activated, so much as an activity, a sequence of chemical actions and changes that result in a particular transcript, modified transcript, and protein; and this last, as we have seen, occupies an array of states often capable of serving multiple purposes. We should analyse the genome into the set of actions it can engage in rather than the set of parts that constitute it.

I have rejected the idea that the material genome is composed of genes for particular phenotypic features. But I should acknowledge that there is a quite different way of understanding the terminology of genes for x, y, etc. As Dawkins explained very clearly in *The Selfish Gene* (1976), when he speaks of a gene for x, say red eyes in a fly, he means any bit of sequence whatever that increases the probability that a fly will have red eyes. An immediate problem, for some a *reductio ad absurdum*, of this proposal is that it suggests that every nucleotide is a gene, often for lots of features. But I don't think this need bother us too much. This account of a gene is well suited to explaining the genetic theory of natural selection as articulated in the mathematical models of population genetics. It is the actual variants in actual genomes that affect the probability of a trait being expressed, given the background genomes and environments that are present in the actual population, that are liable to increase in frequency if a phenotypic feature is being selected for. Frequently these will indeed be single nucleotides. But the great majority of nucleotides will not satisfy the condition just stated.

The problem with this definition is not that it does not do what it is intended for, but that the relativity for being a gene for x to selective context, and a specific, actual population with a specific set of genomes in a specific environment, shows at the least that the status of being a gene for x is a highly relative and unstable one. It is doubtful whether a scientific theory grounded on these evanescent categorisations of DNA provides much contact with real evolutionary processes in the real world (Dupré 1993, pp. 131–142). Similar worries arise with the often-vast numbers of genes identified by genome wide association studies (GWAS) as having a possibly causal relation to phenotypic features of interest, such as non-transmissible diseases. But since this Element is about ontology these issues will not concern us here. Whether population genetics genuinely illuminates our understanding of evolution or whether GWAS give us insight into the causes of disease are strictly epistemological questions. The thousands of distinct genes identified in GWAS investigations of growing numbers of traits are at any rate not an ontologically robust partition of the genome.

I have referred at several points to genes as *coding* for proteins, and it is common to hear the DNA sequence that exists in the genome of an organism described as constituting a code. In some ways, this has been an unfortunate turn of phrase, as it has reinforced the mistaken notion that somehow the parts of the genome represent features of the phenotype (the 'genes for' traits). The complexity of developmental processes, and the intricate relationships between genetic and many other factors in development, make the attempt to trace such relationships generally unproductive (see, e.g., Barnes and Dupré 2008).

As Peter Godfrey-Smith (2000) has argued, it *is* appropriate to treat the DNA sequence as a code, but not for phenotypic traits, only for polypeptide sequences. A central reason for this is that the nature of the relations between nucleotide triplets and amino acids, for example that TAC (Thymine, Adenine, Cytosine) codes for Tyrosine, appears in an interesting sense arbitrary. It seems that the chemistry of the cell could just as easily have been set up to relate this triplet (or 'codon') to any of the other 19 amino acids that make up living proteins. This coding relation points to a real core function of the genome, to provide information about the primary structure (i.e. amino acid sequence) of proteins. However, even this can mislead. Even at this first stage of gene expression, one cannot assume that the nucleotide sequence actually represents the final primary structure of a protein, as there may be a number of editings and splicings between nucleotide sequence and amino acid sequence.

It is crucial to recognise that information can be transferred between generations without being inscribed in some fixed, coding molecule. The idea of a stable, fixed molecule as the container of, on some accounts, all of the developmental information required to build an organism is an attractive one for a substance ontology. The problem of considering an egg, a caterpillar and a butterfly all as temporal stages of the life history of the same individual substance is at least mitigated if the causes of the temporal changes between the stages are intrinsic to the individual. In a sexually reproducing individual, all this information may seem to be assembled at the moment of fertilisation. However, the attractiveness of this solution is reduced when it is appreciated that the developmental sequence will only occur if the organism is exposed to a correct sequence of external conditions, and reduced even further when the organism is seen in many cases to create those external conditions, and to do so in variable ways that respond appropriately to contingencies of the environment. The teleological flavour of these additional aspects of development is embraced by some recent neo-Aristotelians, who embed the teleology in some kind of species-specific essence.

An alternative is that the sequence of generations constitutes a continuous process. While the storage of information, especially with respect to molecules that are not currently active in an organism's metabolism, is very likely essential for life, much of heredity is simply continuity of an ongoing process.[72] This is a perspective encouraged by developmental systems theory (DST), which has insisted that inheritance is grounded in a wide variety of sources, including environment, parental influences that may be learned by imitation, and epigenetic effects, as well as genes (Griffiths and Stotz 1994). DST resonates with a number of themes in contemporary evolutionary biology, including the importance of developmental plasticity (West-Eberhard 2003), the multiple pathways for inheritance (Jablonka and Lamb 2014), and the importance of niche construction, the ways in which organisms alter their environments in order to promote their survival and reproduction (Odling-Smee et al. 2013). Finally, for DST the unit that makes up the evolving lineage is the life history, a history irreducible to a set of interacting ingredients. It is, therefore, a fundamentally processual view of the individual (Griffiths and Stotz 2018).

The view I have presented of biological molecules thus fits seamlessly into the processual view of the organism and the evolving lineage presented earlier in the Element. Life is a hierarchy of processes, and larger scale processes, lineages, both shape and are shaped by the smaller scale processes that constitute them. So at the level of concern to the present section we have seen how the inventory of proteins in a cell is maintained by a range of activities in the cell, and the activity of the genome is affected by a wide range of external factors, mediated by chemical and physical changes to the genome.

The move from a substance-like view of both genes and proteins to a processual view can be seen in both cases in the gradual rejection of a fixed inventory of items of determinate form and function. The paradigm that has driven much molecular biology is that structure determines, and explains, function. Objects are identified and their structure disclosed. From this, eventually, can be inferred the ways they will behave and the ways in which their interactions will generate the behaviour of a larger system (mechanism). But,

---

[72] As, for example, in the transmission of membrane structure in cell division.

first, there is no fixed inventory of things to discover. The inventory is constantly changing, and it is an outcome of the cell's activity not a fixed feature of the cell. Second, structure and function are not asymmetrical in the way this picture supposes. As J. S. Haldane wrote in 1931: 'Structure and functional relation to environment cannot be separated in the serious scientific study of life, since structure expresses the maintenance of function, and function expresses the maintenance of structure' (Haldane 1931). Finding what there is in the cell and describing its structure has been an enormously fruitful strategy for biology. But it must not be forgotten that these are not ontological starting points, but rather factors constantly generated and maintained by the activities of the cell, and factors that describe a situation far from thermodynamical equilibrium, maintained by the cell's metabolism of matter or energy constantly imported into the cell. Both the cell, and the vitally important molecules it contains are, like all else in biology, stabilised processes.

12 Life

Having considered, if briefly, a range of biological entities we are now in a better position to consider the ultimate ontological question in the philosophy of biology, which is, of course, What is life? There is no widely agreed definition that distinguishes the living from the non-living, though the words of Justice Potter Stewart on pornography – 'I know it when I see it' – have some plausibility here. There is one possibly practical question which raises doubts even on this claim, that of how we would recognise some extra-terrestrial entity as living. However, for present purposes an account of what life is on Earth will be ambitious enough.

Many criteria have been advocated for distinguishing the living. These include some or all of homeostasis, metabolism, reproduction, growth, adaptability, and self-organization. In keeping with the dominant place of evolution by natural selection in recent biological thought, some have considered the capacity for this to be the defining feature of life. I find this latter view implausible if only because divine creation of life is very likely false, but surely not incoherent. More generally, as with most concepts of similar breadth, I am sceptical of the project of definition. Our most interesting concepts are dynamic and capable of responding creatively to unanticipated cases. For life, which is constantly evolving new forms, and with a technology that is increasingly capable of replicating many aspects of life, the search for necessary and sufficient conditions seems futile.

More promising is to look at general philosophical perspectives on life. The views I shall discuss, in varying degrees of detail, are vitalism, materialism, mechanism, and organicism. In the end, and to no one's surprise who has read the preceding sections, I shall advocate something close to the last, but more explicitly centred on the idea of life as process, and so named processualism. The natural place to start, however, is with vitalism. Vitalism refers to a long history of views that propose some fundamental difference between living and non-living entities, in some thing or stuff or *élan vital* that is unique to the living, or in laws or principles that apply only to the living.[73] Such views have become extremely unfashionable in recent years, the last more or less mainstream vitalist generally being identified as Hans Driesch in the early twentieth century.

The decline of vitalism is naturally associated with the rise of materialism. Materialism itself, however, remains a much-disputed concept. The part of it that is not so much disputed is the thesis that there are no immaterial stuffs or things, where material is understood as the subject matter of chemistry and physics. Everything made of anything is made of electrons, quarks, etc., and if souls, Gods, or *élans vitals* purport to be made of non-physical stuff, they do not exist. I am happy to subscribe to this thesis, but want to stress how narrow its claim is. It is a claim about what things are made of, and provides no more than weak constraints on what they may be like, how they may behave, or how their features and behaviour may be explained. And there are surely entities – numbers, places, perhaps fields (in the sense from physics)—that are not made of anything. But of course, even the narrow claim is not generally accepted. Most people believe in souls, Gods, ghosts, or other entities that are not supposed to be material in this sense, but have the kind of substantial reality generally associated with material beings. At any rate, within the naturalistic framework that I share with many scientists and most philosophers, the non-existence of the immaterial is widely taken as obvious pending empirical evidence of the existence of some counterexamples.

Materialism is often taken to be strongly associated with the mechanism that I have criticised at various places in this Element. But given the narrowness of the materialist claim as I have construed it, it is quite clear that materialism does not imply mechanism of the kind that has become popular in recent philosophy of science. Mechanism is a thesis about how complex systems work in a material world to generate sophisticated and adaptive behaviour.[74] There is,

---

[73] This dualism of living and non-living should not be confused with the Cartesian distinction between the minded and the material. For Descartes life was material and mechanical. Only humans enjoyed the benefits of a distinct immaterial substance.

[74] Some mechanists, to be sure, insist that their view is about explanation, not about ontology. If the claim is just that some explanations are mechanistic, then I have no disagreement; if the claim is that all explanations are mechanistic, I think it is plainly false (some are, for example, selective, mathematical, functional and, I would say, top-down). Of those that are mechanistic, it is hard to

however, an alternative approach to answering this problem, one that has often been associated with the process ontology advocated in this Element, organicism. This may sound very close to my original description of vitalism, as asserting that different principles apply to living systems and, indeed, the association with vitalism has undoubtedly been used to dismiss versions of organicism. The point of difference is that it is not that there are principles that don't apply to matter, but that these principles apply only when matter is organised in a particular way. Where organicism differs from mechanism is in that it gives a quite different account of the nature of this organisation. It is not a kind of organisation in principle unique to life, though surely nothing we know of that is non-living approximates to the complexity of organisation found in life. It is the peculiar nature of this organisation that I have tried to illustrate and explain in the second part of this Element. At any rate, the reasons that are generally offered for rejecting vitalism have no weight against most versions of this alternative view.

So what is organicism? Here I draw on work by Daniel Nicholson, who has done a lot to recapture a tradition that thrived in the first half of the twentieth century but became much less visible in the second. Two basic premises underlying organicism are, first, that biological theory starts with the organism (Nicholson 2014), and second that the organism exhibits a mode of organisation very different form that of a machine, an organisation which the organicist attempts to articulate (Nicholson 2019).

To the intellectual outsider, the idea that the organism should be at the centre of biology will seem perfectly obvious. Surely wallabies, willows and wagtails are what biology is about? But as Evelyn Fox Keller describes in her book, *The Century of the Gene* (2002), in the twentieth century the organism came to be seen as much less central to biology than the gene. One reason for this, as we have seen in the preceding section, is that especially in the second half of the century, the features of the organism came to be seen as entirely dependent on the properties of genes, or on the running of the genetic program. This kind of strong genetic reductionism has been largely rejected. But a more subtle reason was the separation of soma and germline proposed by Weismann at the beginning of the century. This has increasingly been taken to mean that evolution should be understood as affecting genes, transmitted through the germline, whereas the soma (the rest of the organism), leaving no lasting mark on evolutionary history, could be ignored from a theoretical point of view.

---

see that they could be explanatory without there being some real structure at least strongly isomorphic to the explanatorily proposed mechanism.

One might immediately object that organisms do have a lasting evolutionary effect, as it is their more or less well adapted characteristics that determine whether they survive and reproduce. But this response can be negated by the idea that the characteristics of the organism are in fact determined by the environment through an optimising selective process. The organism is thus reduced to a device that mediates between genes and environment, to maximise the success of the genes. This is the picture that reached its definitive articulation in Richard Dawkins (1976) classic work: 'lumbering robots' (organisms) merely serve the aims (growth in frequency) of their masters and controllers, the genes.

This picture has, however, been largely dismantled in recent years by the development of more sophisticated models of evolution, as summarised in the Extended Evolutionary Synthesis briefly summarised in Section 6. The recognition of niche construction (Odling-Smee et al. 2013) undermines the idea of the organism's traits merely responding to a given environment; extended inheritance (Jablonka and Lamb 2014) points to a much more complex development not fully determined by genes; evo-devo (Müller 2007) explores the influence of historical inertia, as embedded in evolved developmental trajectories, in limiting and channelling the possibilities for adaptation; and developmental plasticity (West Eberhard 2003) highlights the role of the organism as an agent in its own adaptive change.

More important from a metaphysical point of view, however, is the second organicist thesis, that the organism is not a machine and, of course, the outlines of an alternative view of the way matter is organised to form living systems. The central reason for both the negative and positive aspects of this difference that I have stressed throughout this Element, is that the organism is a process. Whereas a machine can be switched off and put away while it is not needed, an organism, as is the defining characteristic of a process, must continue countless activities to continue to exist. Moreover, as a stabilised, persistent process, activity is not merely a trivial, definitional necessity, but a causal necessity. Whereas a mechanism starts with a given structure that generates activity through the interactions of its parts, for an organism, qua persistent process, vast numbers of activities are required to maintain that structure.

Furthermore, a machine is invariably understood in a strictly bottom-up way: the behaviour of the whole is a result of the behaviours of its parts. By contrast, the stabilisation of an organism is not merely bottom-up, through the behaviours of its constituents, but also top-down, through the constraints exerted by the whole on the behaviours of the parts. Think of the relation between an organism and an organ, say a heart. The heart is essential to the survival of the organism in familiar ways, but not only are lungs arteries, kidneys, etc., essential to the survival of the heart, but so is the activity of the organism in moving around the world finding nutrition. The relation between the organism and the lineage to which it belongs can be described similarly. In this case natural selection can be seen as a process that maintains the survivability of the organisms that make up the lineage, while also stabilising the lineage by determining which organisms are allowed to be part of it (Dupré 2017). Or compare the maintenance of the optimal proteome discussed in section 10.

This points to the picture of life that I wish to advocate. Life is a hierarchy of processes. Each level of the hierarchy consists of processes that persist because they are stabilised both by processes at lower levels and their embedding in higher level processes. Cells, for example, are stabilised both by molecular processes internal to them and by their relations to other cells in larger systems, such as multicellular organisms. At the bottom of this hierarchy (if there is one: it is at least a metaphysical possibility that everything is composed of smaller things) are non-living processes. Perhaps these – the entities of fundamental physics – are not processes but substances. This is a question thankfully beyond the remit of this Element though, as noted earlier, it seems to me much more plausible that they are processes. But life, at any rate, wherever it emerges, is processual.

The highest level of the hierarchy might be either a level at which there is no stability, or it might be a stabilised entity that has minimal external interactions. The latter possibility is promoted by advocates of the Gaia hypothesis, in which Gaia, the entire terrestrial biosphere, is a stabilised entity depending ultimately on nothing beyond the flux of energy from the sun (Lovelock 2000). At the opposite extreme are those who consider phenomena above the level of the lineage merely an upshot of the activities of lineages. Ecosystems, in particular, might be no more than the summation of the reproductive and ecological activities of the members of lineages, and so-called Gaia no more than the totality of these ecosystems. I won't attempt to adjudicate this issue here. Whether we consider the totality of terrestrial life itself to be some kind of living system I interpret as the question whether this totality constitutes some kind of stabilised or self-organising system. Cells, organs, and organisms are clearly living systems that meet this condition. Molecules are not, though perhaps aggregates such as the proteome or the transcriptome would count. Gaia is a debated case, debated because it is not agreed whether the totality of terrestrial life constitutes such a system. If the status of Gaia matters, it is because, recalling the argument of Section 3, if Gaia is part of the hierarchy of living systems, it very likely has downward causal influence on its constitutive lineages and organisms. If human activities disrupt the stability of Gaia, this may well have effects on us and they may not be good (Lovelock 2007).

As an interesting test case near the other end of the hierarchy, we might look at the virus. An individual virus particle does not itself appear to be a stabilised system. If we think of the virion, the inactive particle that constitutes the virus external to its host, its persistence is more like that of a table than that of a cell. Its parts cohere until something dissolves the bonds between them.[75] However, I think this is the wrong way to think of the virus. The virion is not the virus, but a stage in the life cycle of the virus. At certain stages of its life cycle, in its engagement with the host cell, there may actually be no unique physical entity at all that constitutes the virus; there are just the chemical activities that it initiates in its engagement with the cell (Dupré and Güttinger 2016). But clearly this does not mean the virus has ceased to exist. What persists throughout this engagement is the process that maintains the viral lineage. The lineage, in this case, is only partly composed of discrete entities. Given this lineage-forming process, stabilised both by the chemical activities within the infected cell and by whatever higher level (e.g. selective) processes are necessary for its persistence, I am inclined to call the viral flow a living process. But perhaps a more important message is that the boundary between the living and the non-living is not a sharp one (Dupré and O'Malley 2009). The points at which the hierarchy of processes becomes, and ceases to be, living are not sharply defined.

I should finally note, repeating a point I made in section two, that I do not mean the idea of hierarchy to be taken too seriously. I do not think there is a determinate number of levels in nature or that all entities belong to a specific level. Is the circulatory system an organ, or a level intermediate between the organ and the organism comprising an assembly of organs (such as the heart and the arteries) and stuff (the blood)? Do such stuffs as blood or lymph belong in the hierarchy at all? Is a composite organism such as a lichen or a coral at a higher level than its component organisms? These questions should not detain us and we should not expect them to be answered by Nature. The point is rather that to understand a biological entity as the kind of active being it is we need to understand both the internal activities and interactions that enable its persistence, but also its more or less obligatory interactions with its wider environment. It is often natural and even useful to think of this fact in terms of a hierarchy. But we should not put any weight on the specific assignment of elements to positions in such a hierarchy.

So life, I claim, is composed of a multitude of mutually sustaining processes at a range of spatial and temporal scales. The term 'organicism', useful as it is in distinguishing the position from both mechanism and vitalism, and even though

---

[75] It is of course possible to see these bonds as ultimately processual at the level of physical or chemical activity. But this, again, is a question about the ontology of the sub-biological that I won't go into here.

its leading exponents have been convinced processualists, does not seem ideally suited to name such a position. Although the organism is perhaps the central focus of human interest in the living, I am not convinced that it has a special ontological status. This is particularly so in view of the difficulties in defining the organism itself noted in Section 8. This should remind us again that the hierarchy itself has elements of vagueness. With the possible exception of the cell, what constitutes an individual at each level is not typically a question with a precise answer. The point of organicism in the present discussion is more negative than positive: the denial that a particular level, the physical or the genetic, has a privileged status; and the denial that a particular organisation (mechanical), properly characterises the living.

Despite the strong affinities of my views with the organicist tradition, I am inclined to prefer the term 'processualism', except that that has no obvious special connection to life, so perhaps it would have to be 'biological processualism'. But then there is nothing specifically biological about mechanism or, still less, materialism. Indeed, the point of these words is in large part to deny that there is something special about life in the way that vitalists maintain. That vitalism attributes the wrong kind of specialness to life, at least, is something that materialists, mechanists and organicists can all agree. If, as I believe, if tentatively, the whole world is processual, processualism, like mechanism and materialism, will ontologically unify life with the rest of existence. Or if, as organicists maintained, it turns out that there are deep features of the processes of life that are unique to living systems, then the term processualism will serve to mark that dualism.

Let me conclude with a brief comment on a topic that may have impressed by its absence, teleology. One feature of life that has convinced some that it is fundamentally different from the non-living is the apparent goal-directedness of biological systems. Machines have goals or purposes, because that is how we designed and constructed them. If we are not purposive machines created by a divine being, then where does this inescapable sense of purposiveness in life come from? The traditional materialist answer, of course, is natural selection, which is taken to have built machines in much the way God had previously been supposed to have done: selecting for survival-promoting traits has produced organisms that seem to be deeply committed to the end of survival.

After criticising Richard Dawkins at several points in this Element, let me address the question of purpose by way of a phrase from his classic book that I think is truly illuminating. On p. 13 of *The Selfish Gene* (1976) he writes that 'Darwin's "survival of the fittest" is really a special case of a more general law of *survival of the stable*.' He goes on to illustrate this with cases of such stable entities as atoms and mountains. But as I have stressed throughout this Element, there are two ways of being stable. One is by default, by doing nothing. The universe predicted in some models of ultimate heat death would perhaps be the most stable object possible; atoms and rocks do a good job. But there is also stability by activity, the stability of persistent processes illustrated by river eddies and thunderstorms but also, far more interestingly, by life.

Both organisms and lineages exist because they are stable, and their mutually conditioned stability is what evolution makes possible. Machines, as every car owner knows, are not very stable. Their parts degrade, eventually to the point where it is no longer worth replacing them; no machines are very stable without regular intervention, or maintenance. Life has found a quite different, perhaps better, way of being stable. First, by regeneration and self-repair of parts, some organisms can live for very long times, some plants for thousands of years. But second, by virtue of the nested hierarchy of living systems, life itself is stable over billions of years. The human lineage, like all others, goes back several billion years. This stability is made possible by a hierarchy of processes – evolutionary, developmental, metabolic, and so on. Their contribution to stabilisation and, in the case of organisms, reproduction, looks inescapably teleological as it seems designed to maintain some element of the system or hierarchy. But this is just how stabilisation works in a world of process. So, ultimately, nothing but the survival of the stable is required to explain the emergence of a living world with all the extraordinary purposiveness of our own.

Bibliography

Anderson, J. M. 2000. 'Multinucleated Giant Cells', *Current Opinion in Hematology*, 7, 40–7.

Ankeny, R. A. and S. Leonelli 2011. 'What's so Special about Model Organisms', *Studies in History and Philosophy of Science Part A*, 42, 313–23.

Austin, J. L. 1962. *Sense and Sensibilia* (Oxford: Oxford University Press).

Austin, C. J. 2020. 'Organisms, Activity, and Being: On the Substance of Process Ontology', *European Journal for Philosophy of Science*, 10(2), 1–21.

Balch, W. E., R. I. Morimoto, A. Dillin and J. W. Kelly 2008. 'Adapting Proteostasis for Disease Intervention', *Science*, 319, 916–19.

Bapteste, E., M. A. O'Malley, R. Beiko et al. 2009. 'Prokaryotic Evolution and the Tree of Life are Two Different Things', *Biology Direct*, 4, 34.

Bateson, P. N. Cartwright, J. Dupré, K. Laland and D. Noble (eds.) 2017. Special Issue on 'New Trends in Evolutionary Biology: Biological, Philosophical and Social Science'.

Barker, M. J. 2010. 'Species Intrinsicalism', *Philosophy of Science*, 77, 73–91.

Barnes, B. and J. Dupré 2008. *Genomes and What to Make of Them* (Chicago: University of Chicago Press).

Beatty, J. 1995. 'The Evolutionary Contingency Thesis', in G. Wolters, and J. G. Lennox, (eds.). *Concepts, Theories, and Rationality in the Biological Sciences* (Pittsburgh: University of Pittsburgh Press) 45–81.

Bedau, M. 1997. 'Weak Emergence', *Philosophical Perspectives*, 11, 375–99.

Borges, J. L. 1998. 'On the exactitude of science', translated by Andrew Hurley in *Collected Fictions* (New York: Penguin) 325.

Brandon, R. 1997. 'Does Biology Have Laws? The Experimental Evidence', *Philosophy of Science*, 64, S444–S457.

Burkhardt, R. W. 2013. 'Lamarck, Evolution, and the Inheritance of Acquired Characters', *Genetics*, 194(4), 793–805.

Cartwright, N. 1983. *How the Laws of Physics Lie* (Oxford: Oxford University Press).

Cartwright, N. 1999. *The Dappled World: A Study of the Boundaries of Science* (Cambridge: Cambridge University Press).

Craver, C. F. 2007. *Explaining the Brain: Mechanisms and the Mosaic Unity of Neuroscience* (Oxford: Oxford University Press).

Craver, C. F. and W. Bechtel 2007. 'Top-Down Causation without Top-Down Causes', *Biology and Philosophy*, 22(4), 547–63.

Craver, C. and J. Tabery, 2019. 'Mechanisms in Science', *The Stanford Encyclopedia of Philosophy* (Summer 2019 Ed.), E. N. Zalta (ed.), URL = https://plato.stanford.edu/archives/sum2019/entries/science-mechanisms/>.

Dawkins, R. 1976. *The Selfish Gene* (Oxford: Oxford University Press).

Dawkins, R. 1996. *The Blind Watchmaker: Why the Evidence of Evolution Reveals a Universe without Design* (New York: W. W. Norton & Company).

Dennett, D. C. 1996. *Darwin's Dangerous Idea: Evolution and the Meaning of Life* (New York: Simon and Schuster).

Devitt, M. 2008. 'Resurrecting Biological Essentialism', *Philosophy of Science*, 75, 344–82.

Devitt, M. 2010. 'Species Have (Partly) Intrinsic Essences', *Philosophy of Science*, 77, 648–61.

Devitt, M. 2021. 'Defending Intrinsic Biological Essentialism'. *Philosophy of Science*, 88, 67–82.

Dobzhansky, T. 1973. 'Nothing in Biology Makes Sense Except in the Light of Evolution', *The American Biology Teacher*, 35, 125–9.

Donlan, R. M. 2002. 'Biofilms: Microbial Life on Surfaces', *Emerging Infectious Diseases*, 8(9), 881.

Doolittle, W. F. and A. Booth 2017. 'It's the Song, not the Singer: An Exploration of Holobiosis and Evolutionary Theory', *Biology & Philosophy*, 32(1), 5–24.

Doolittle, W. F. and S. A. Inkpen 2018. 'Processes and Patterns of Interaction as Units of Selection: An Introduction to ITSNTS Thinking', *Proceedings of the National Academy of Sciences*, 115(16), 4006–14.

Doolittle, W. F. 2019. 'Speciation without Species: A Final Word', *Philosophy, Theory, and Practice in Biology*, 11.

Dupre, J. 1993. *The Disorder of Things: Metaphysical Foundations of the Disunity of Science* (Cambridge MA: Harvard University Press).

Dupré, J. 1999. 'On the Impossibility of a Monistic Account of Species', in R. A. Wilson (ed.) *Species: New Interdisciplinary Essays* (Cambridge MA.: MIT Press) 3–20.

Dupré, J. 2001. 'In Defence of Classification', *Studies in The History and Philosophy of the Biological and Biomedical Sciences*, 32, 203–19.

Dupré, J. 2010. 'The Polygenomic Organism', in S. Parry and J. Dupré (eds.) *Nature After the Genome* (Oxford: Blackwell) 19–31. Reprinted in Dupré 2012.

Dupré, J. 2012. *Processes of Life* (Oxford: Oxford University Press).

Dupré, J. 2013. 'Living Causes', in *Aristotelian Society Supplementary Volume*, 87 (Oxford: Oxford University Press) 19–37.

Dupré, J. 2017. 'The Metaphysics of Evolution', *Interface Focus*. Published online, 18 August, 2017. http://rsfs.royalsocietypublishing.org/content/7/5/20160148\

Dupré, J. and S. Güttinger 2016. 'Viruses as Living Processes', *Studies in History and Philosophy of Biological and Biomedical Sciences*, 59, 109–16.

Dupré, J. and D. J. Nicholson 2018. 'A Manifesto for a Processual Philosophy of Biology', in Nicholson and Dupré, 2018, 3–45.

Dupré, J. and M. A. O'Malley 2009. 'Varieties of Living Things: Life at the Intersection of Lineage and Metabolism', *Philosophy and Theory in Biology*, 1. http://dx.doi.org/10.3998/ptb.6959004.0001.003

Elias, S. and Banin, E. 2012. 'Multi-Species Biofilms: Living with Friendly Neighbors', *FEMS Microbiology Reviews*, 36(5), 990–1004.

Ereshefsky, M. 1992. 'Eliminative pluralism', *Philosophy of Science*, 59(4), 671–90.

Ereshefsky, M. 2010. 'What's Wrong with the New Biological Essentialism', *Philosophy of Science*, 77, 674–85.

Ereshefsky, M. and M. Pedroso 2013. 'Biological Individuality: The Case of Biofilms', *Biology and Philosophy*, 28(2), 331–49.

Forgacs, G. and S. A. Newman 2005. *Biological Physics of the Developing Embryo* (Cambridge: Cambridge University Press).

Frigg, R. and S. Hartmann 2018. 'Models in Science', *The Stanford Encyclopedia of Philosophy* (Summer 2018 Ed.), E. N. Zalta (ed.), URL = https://plato.stanford.edu/archives/sum2018/entries/models-science/.

Gilbert, S. F. and D. Epel 2015. *Ecological Developmental Biology: The Environmental Regulation of Development, Health, and Evolution* (Sunderland, MA.: Sinauer Associates).

Ghiselin, M. T. 1974. 'A Radical Solution to the Species Problem', *Systematic Biology*, 23(4), 536–44.

Glennan, S. S. 1996. 'Mechanisms and the Nature of Causation', *Erkenntnis*, 44(1), 49–71.

Glennan, S. and P. Illari (eds.) 2017. *The Routledge Handbook of Mechanisms and Mechanical Philosophy* (Abingdon, UK: Taylor & Francis).

Godfrey-Smith, P. 2000. 'On the Theoretical Role of "Genetic Coding"', *Philosophy of Science*, 67(1), 26–44.

Godfrey-Smith, P. 2009. *Darwinian Populations and Natural Selection* (New York: Oxford University Press).

Godfrey-Smith P. 2015. 'Reproduction, Symbiosis and the Eukaryotic Cell', *Proceedings of the National Academy of Sciences USA*, 112(33), 10120–5.

Green, S. and R. Batterman (2017). 'Biology meets Physics: Reductionism and Multi-scale Modelling of Morphogenesis', *Studies in History and Philosophy of the Biological and Biomedical Sciences*, 61, 20–34.

Griffiths, P. E. 1999. 'Squaring the Circle: Natural Kinds with Historical Essences', in R. A. Wilson (ed.) *Species: New Interdisciplinary Essays* (Cambridge, MA.: MIT Press) 209–28.

Griffiths, P. E. and R. D. Gray 1994. 'Developmental Systems and Evolutionary Explanation', *The Journal of Philosophy*, 91(6), 277–304.

Griffiths, P. E. and K. Stotz 2018. 'Developmental Systems Theory as Process Theory', in Nicholson and Dupré, 2018, 225–45.

Guay A and T. Pradeu (eds.) 2015a. *Individuals Across the Sciences* (New York: Oxford University Press).

Guay, A., and Pradeu, T. 2015b. 'To Be Continued: The Genidentity of Physical and Biological Processes', in Guay and Pradeu (2015a), 317–47.

Güttinger, S. 2018. 'A Process Ontology for Macromolecular Biology', in Nicholson and Dupré (2018), 303–20.

Güttinger, S. and J. Dupré 2016. 'Genomics and Postgenomics', *The Stanford Encyclopedia of Philosophy* (Winter 2016 Ed.), E. N. Zalta (ed.), URL = https://plato.stanford.edu/archives/win2016/entries/genomics/.

Hacking, I. 2007. 'Natural Kinds: Rosy Dawn, Scholastic Twilight', *Royal Institute of Philosophy Supplements*, 61, 203–39.

Haldane, J. S. 1931. *The Philosophical Basis of Biology* (London: Hodder and Stoughton).

Haldane, J. B. S. 1963. 'Review of The Truth About Death', *Journal of Genetics*, 58, 464.

Harré, R. and E. Madden 1975. *Causal Powers: A Theory of Natural Necessity* (Oxford: Blackwell).

Hull, D. L. 1976. 'Are Species Really Individuals?', *Systematic Zoology*, 25(2), 174–91.

Hull, D. L. 1980. 'Individuality and Selection', *Annual Review of Ecology and Systematics*, 11: 311–32.

Humphreys, P. 2016. *Emergence* (Oxford: Oxford University Press).

Jablonka, E. and M. J. Lamb 2014. *Evolution in Four Dimensions: Genetic, Epigenetic, Behavioral, and Symbolic Variation in the History of Life* (revised ed.) (Cambridge, MA.: MIT press).

Jablonka, E., and Raz, G. (2009). 'Transgenerational Epigenetic Inheritance: Prevalence, Mechanisms, and Implications for the Study of Heredity and Evolution', *The Quarterly Review of Biology*, 84(2), 131–76.

Jeffery, C. J. 1999. 'Moonlighting Proteins', *Trends in Biochemical Sciences*, 24(1), 8–11.

Jeffery, C. J. 2009. 'Moonlighting Proteins – an Update', *Molecular BioSystems*, 5(4), 345–50.

Keller, E. F. 2009. *The Century of the Gene.* (Cambridge, MA.: Harvard University Press).

Kim, J. 2000. *Mind in a Physical World: An Essay on the Mind-Body Problem and Mental Causation* (Cambridge, MA.: MIT press).

Kingma, E. 2019. 'Were You a Part of your Mother?', *Mind*, 128(511), 609–46.

Kitcher, P. 1982. *Abusing Science: The Case against Creationism* (Cambridge, MA.: MIT press).

Koshland Jr, D. E. 1958. 'Application of a Theory of Enzyme Specificity to Protein Synthesis', *Proceedings of the National Academy of Sciences of the United States of America*, 44(2), 98.

Laland, K. N., T. Uller, M. W. Feldman, K. et al. 2015. 'The Extended Evolutionary Synthesis: Its Structure, Assumptions and Predictions', *Proceedings of the Royal Society B: Biological Sciences*, 282, 20151019.

Lamarck, J. B. 1984/1809. *Zoological Philosophy: An Exposition with Regard to the Natural History of Animals, tr.* Hugh Elliot (Chicago: University of Chicago Press).

Lavialle, C., G. Cornelis, A. Dupressoir, C. et al. 2013. 'Paleovirology of "Syncytins", Retroviral Env Genes Exapted for a Role in Placentation', *Philosophical Transactions of the Royal Society of London. Series B, Biological Sciences*, 368(1626), 20120507. https://doi.org/10.1098/rstb .2012.0507

Leslie, S.-J. 2013. 'Essence and Natural Kinds: When Science Meets Preschooler Intuition', in T. S. Gendler and J. Hawthorne (eds.), *Oxford Studies in Epistemology Volume 4* (Oxford: Oxford University Press) 108–65.

Lewin, K. 1922. *Der Begriff der Genese in Physik, Biologie und Entwicklungsgeschichte: eine Untersuchung zur vergleichenden Wissenschaftslehre* (Berlin: Springer).

Lewis, D. K. 1973. 'Causation', *Journal of Philosophy*, 70, 556–67.

Lloyd, E. A. 1988. *The Structure and Confirmation of Evolutionary Theory* (New York: Greenwood Press).

Lloyd, E. A. 2020. 'Units and Levels of Selection', *The Stanford Encyclopedia of Philosophy* (Spring 2020 Ed.), E. N. Zalta (ed.), URL = https://plato .stanford.edu/archives/spr2020/entries/selection-units/.

Lloyd E. A. 2017. 'Holobionts as Units of Selection: Holobionts as Interactors, Reproducers, and Manifestors of Adaptation', in S. B. Gissis, E. Lamm and A. Shavit (eds.), *Landscapes of Collectivity in the Life Sciences* (Cambridge, MA.: MIT press), 351–67.

Lovelock, J. 2000. *Gaia: A New Look at Life on Earth.* Oxford: Oxford University Press.

Lovelock, J. 2007. *The Revenge of Gaia: Why the Earth is Fighting Back and How We Can Still Save Humanity* (London: Penguin).

Machamer, P. K., L. Darden, and C. F. Craver 2000. 'Thinking about Mechanisms', *Philosophy of Science*, 67, 1–25.

Mallet, J., N. Besansky, and M. W. Hahn 2016. 'How Reticulated are Species?', *BioEssays*, 38, 140–9.

Mammoto, T. and D. E. Ingber 2010. 'Mechanical Control of Tissue and Organ Development', *Development*, 137(9), 1407–20.

Mayden, R. L. 1997. 'A Hierarchy of Species Concepts: The Denouement in the Saga of the Species Problem', in M. F. Claridge, H. A. Dawah and M. R. Wilson (eds.), *Species: The Units of Diversity* (London: Chapman & Hall), 381–423.

Mayr, E. 1982. *The Growth of Biological Thought: Diversity, Evolution and Inheritance* (Cambridge, MA.: Harvard University Press).

Mackie, J. L. 1974. *The Cement of the Universe: A Study of Causation* (Oxford: Clarendon Press).

Meincke, A. S. 2019. 'The Disappearance of Change: Towards a Process Account of Persistence', *International Journal of Philosophical Studies*, 27(1), 12–30.

Meincke, A. S. 2020. 'Processual Animalism: Towards a Scientifically Informed Theory of Personal Identity', in Meincke and Dupré 2020.

Meincke, A. S. and J. Dupré (eds.) 2020. *Biological Identity: Perspectives from Metaphysics and the Philosophy of Biology* (Abingdon, UK: Routledge).

Meincke, A. S. forthcoming. 'A Process View of Pregnancy'.

Mill, J. S. 1872/1843. *A System of Logic, Ratiocinative and Inductive: Being a Connected View of the Principles of Evidence and the Methods of Scientific Investigation*, 8th ed. (London: Longmans, Green).

Millstein, R. L. 2009. 'Populations as Individuals', *Biological Theory*, 4(3), 267–73.

Moraes, S. S., L. W. Cardoso, K. L. Silva-Brandão and M. Duarte 2017. 'Extreme Sexual Dimorphism and Polymorphism in Two Species of the Tiger Moth Genus *Dysschema* (Lepidoptera: Erebidae): Association between Males and Females, Sexual Mimicry and Melanism Revealed by Integrative Taxonomy', *Systematics and Biodiversity*, 15(3), 259–73.

Moran N. and D. B. Sloan 2015. 'The Hologenome Concept: Helpful or Hollow?', *PLoS Biology*, 13(12), e1002311.

Morgan, M. 1999. 'Learning from Models', in M. Morgan and M. Morrison (eds.) *Models as Mediators. Perspectives on Natural and Social Science* (Cambridge: Cambridge University Press), 347–88.

Müller, G. B. 2007. 'Evo–Devo: Extending the Evolutionary Synthesis', *Nature Reviews Genetics*, 8(12), 943–9.

Mumford, S. and R. L. Anjum 2011. *Getting Causes from Powers* (Oxford: Oxford University Press).

Newman, S. A. 2020. 'The Origins and Evolution of Animal Identity'. In Meincke and Dupré, 2020, 128–48.

Nelson, K. E., et al. 'Evidence for Lateral Gene Transfer between Archaea and Bacteria from Genome Sequence of Thermotoga maritima', *Nature*, 399.6734, 323–9.

Nicholson, D. J. 2010. 'Biological Atomism and Cell Theory', *Studies in History and Philosophy of Biological and Biomedical Sciences*, 41(3), 202–11.

Nicholson, D. J. 2012. 'The Concept of Mechanism in Biology', *Studies in History and Philosophy of Biological and Biomedical Sciences*, 43(1), 152–63.

Nicholson, D. J. 2014. 'The Return of the Organism as a Fundamental Explanatory Concept in Biology', *Philosophy Compass*, 9(5), 347–59.

Nicholson, D. J. 2018. 'Reconceptualizing the Organism: From Complex Machine to Flowing Stream', in Nicholson and Dupré 2018, 139–66.

Nicholson, D. J. 2019. 'Is the Cell Really a Machine?', *Journal of Theoretical Biology*, 477: 108–26.

Nicholson, D. J and J. Dupré 2018. *Everything Flows: Towards a Processual Philosophy of Biology* (Oxford: Oxford University Press).

Nicholson, D. J. and R. Gawne 2015. 'Neither Logical Empiricism nor Vitalism, but Organicism: What the Philosophy of Biology Was', *History and Philosophy of the Life Sciences*, 37(4), 345–81.

Odling-Smee, F. J., K. N. Laland and M. W. Feldman 2013. *Niche Construction: The Neglected Process in Evolution* (Princeton, NJ: Princeton University Press).

Okasha, S. 2006. *Evolution and the Levels of Selection* (Oxford: Oxford University Press).

Okasha, S. 2020. 'On the very idea of biological individuality', talk at LSE, 25 February, 2020.

O'Malley, M. A. 2017. 'From Endosymbiosis to Holobionts: Evaluating a Conceptual Legacy', *Journal of Theoretical Biology*, 434, 34–41.

O'Malley, M. A. and J. Dupré. 2007. 'Size doesn't matter: towards a more inclusive philosophy of biology', *Biology and Philosophy*, 22, 155–191.

Paluch, E. and C. P. Heisenberg 2009. 'Biology and Physics of Cell Shape Changes in Development', *Current Biology*, 19(17), R790–R799.

Pradeu, T. 2018. 'Genidentity and Biological Processes' in Nicholson and Dupré 2018, 96–112.

Putnam, H. 1975. *Mind, Language and Reality* (Cambridge: Cambridge University Press).

Rak, R., O. Dahan and Y. Pilpel 2018. 'Repertoires of tRNAs: The Couplers of Genomics and Proteomics', *Annual Review of Cell and Developmental Biology*, 34, 239–64.

Reiss, J. 2009. *Not by Design: Retiring Darwin's Watchmaker* (Berkeley, CA.: University of California Press).

Rescher, N. 2006. *Process Ontological Deliberations* (Frankfurt: Ontos).

Rodgers, A. B., C. P. Morgan, N. A. Leu, and T. L. Bale 2015. 'Transgenerational Epigenetic Programming via Sperm MicroRNA Recapitulates Effects of Paternal Stress', *Proceedings of the National Academy of Sciences*, 112(44), 13699–704.

Robinson, H. 2020. 'Substance', *The Stanford Encyclopedia of Philosophy* (Spring 2020 Ed.), Edward N. Zalta (ed.), URL = https://plato.stanford.edu /archives/spr2020/entries/substance/.

Roper, M., C. Ellison, J. W. Taylor and N. L. Glass 2011. 'Nuclear and Genome Dynamics in Multinucleate Ascomycete Fungi', *Current Biology*, 21(18), R786–R793.

Roughgarden, J., S. F. Gilbert, E. Rosenberg, I. Zilber-Rosenberg, and E. A. Lloyd 2018. 'Holobionts as Units of Selection and a Model of their Population Dynamics and Evolution', *Biological Theory*, 13, 44–65.

Salmon, W. 1984. *Scientific Explanation and the Causal Structure of the World* (Princeton, NJ: Princeton University Press).

Schrödinger, E. 1944. *What is Life?* (Cambridge: Cambridge University Press).

Sivan E. and E. Banin 2012. 'Multi-species Biofilms: Living with Friendly Neighbors', *FEMS Microbiology Reviews*, 36, 990–1004.

Ruse, M. 2019. *The Darwinian Revolution* (Cambridge: Cambridge University Press).

Shapiro, J. A. 2005. 'A 21st Century View of Evolution: Genome System Architecture, Repetitive DNA, and Natural Genetic Engineering', *Gene*, 345(1), 91–100.

Shapiro, J. A. 2017. 'Biological Action in Read–Write Genome Evolution', *Interface Focus*, 7(5), 20160115.

Smith, B. and D. M. Mark 2003. 'Do Mountains Exist? Towards an Ontology of Landforms', *Environment and Planning B: Planning and Design*, 30(3), 411–27.

Sober, E. and D. S. Wilson 1999. *Unto Others: The Evolution and Psychology of Unselfish Behavior* (Cambridge, MA.: Harvard University Press).

Stein, R. L. 2004. 'Towards a Process Philosophy of Chemistry', *Hyle: International Journal for Philosophy of Chemistry*, 10(4), 5–22.

Stein, R. L. 2006. 'A Process Theory of Enzyme Catalytic Power – The Interplay of Science and Metaphysics', *Foundations of Chemistry*, 8, 3–29.

Stein, R. L. 2020. 'Mechanisms of Macromolecular Reactions', in press.

Steward, H. 2020. 'Substances, Agents and Processes', *Philosophy*, 95 (1), 41–61.

Stout, R. 2016. 'The Category of Occurrent Continuants', *Mind*, 125(497), 41–62.

Suárez, J. 2020. 'The Stability of Traits Conception of the Hologenome: An Evolutionary Account of Holobiont Individuality', *History and Philosophy of the Life Sciences*, 42(1), 1–27.

Suárez, J. 2018. 'The Importance of Symbiosis in Philosophy of Biology: An Analysis of the Current Debate on Biological Individuality and its Historical Roots', *Symbiosis*, 76(2), 77–96.

Toon, A. 2012. *Models as Make-Believe: Imagination, Fiction and Scientific Representation* (Basingstoke: Palgrave Macmillan).

Weisberg, M. 2012. *Simulation and Similarity: Using Models to Understand the World* (New York: Oxford University Press).

West-Eberhard, M. J. 2003. *Developmental Plasticity and Evolution* (New York: Oxford University Press).

Wiggins, D. 2016. 'Activity, Process, Continuant, Substance, Organism', *Philosophy*, 91: 269–80. Reprinted in Meincke and Dupré 2020.

Wilson, J. 2016. 'Metaphysical Emergence: Weak and Strong', in T. Bigaj and C. Wüthrich (eds.), *Metaphysics in Contemporary Physics* (Leiden, The Netherlands: Brill | Rodopi).

Wilson, R. A. and M. J. Barker 2019. 'Biological Individuals', *The Stanford Encyclopedia of Philosophy* (Fall 2019 Ed.), E. N. Zalta (ed.), URL = https://plato.stanford.edu/archives/fall2019/entries/biology-individual/.

Wimsatt, W. K. 2007. *Re-engineering Philosophy for Limited Beings: Piecewise Approximations to Reality* (Cambridge, MA.: Harvard University Press).

Winther, R. G. 2016. 'The Structure of Scientific Theories', *The Stanford Encyclopedia of Philosophy* (Winter 2016 Ed.), E. N. Zalta (ed.), URL = https://plato.stanford.edu/archives/win2016/entries/structure-scientific-theories/.

Woodward, J. 2003. *Making Things Happen: A Theory of Causal Explanation* (New York: Oxford University Press).

Wu, Q., S. G. Medina, G. Kushawah, et al. 2019. 'Translation Affects mRNA Stability in a Codon-Dependent Manner in Human Cells', *Elife*, 8, e45396.

Acknowledgements

I would like to thank the European Research Council, which funded much of the research on which this Element was based under the European Union's Seventh Framework Programme (FP7/2007–2013), ERC Grant Agreement 324186. I would like to thank Stephan Güttinger, Anne Sophie Meincke and Daniel Nicholson, who were research fellows on this grant, and made major contributions to my thinking on most of the issues discussed herein. I also thank Gabe Dupré, Sabina Leonelli and two anonymous referees. All these people have made detailed comments on the text, which have improved it immeasurably.

Cambridge Elements ☰

Elements in the Philosophy of Biology

Grant Ramsey
KU Leuven
Grant Ramsey is a BOFZAP research professor at the Institute of Philosophy, KU Leuven, Belgium. His work centers on philosophical problems at the foundation of evolutionary biology. He has been awarded the Popper Prize twice for his work in this area. He also publishes in the philosophy of animal behavior, human nature and the moral emotions. He runs the Ramsey Lab (theramseylab.org), a highly collaborative research group focused on issues in the philosophy of the life sciences.

Michael Ruse
Florida State University
Michael Ruse is the Lucyle T. Werkmeister Professor of Philosophy and the Director of the Program in the History and Philosophy of Science at Florida State University. He is Professor Emeritus at the University of Guelph, in Ontario, Canada. He is a former Guggenheim fellow and Gifford lecturer. He is the author or editor of over sixty books, most recently *Darwinism as Religion: What Literature Tells Us about Evolution; On Purpose; The Problem of War: Darwinism, Christianity, and their Battle to Understand Human Conflict;* and *A Meaning to Life.*

About the Series

This Cambridge Elements series provides concise and structured introductions to all of the central topics in the philosophy of biology. Contributors to the series are cutting-edge researchers who offer balanced, comprehensive coverage of multiple perspectives, while also developing new ideas and arguments from a unique viewpoint.

Cambridge Elements ☰

Philosophy of Biology

A full series listing is available at www.cambridge.org/EPBY

Printed in the United States
by Baker & Taylor Publisher Services